KU-509-318

GENE KERRIGAN

Never Make a Promise You Can't Break

How to Succeed in Irish Politics

Gill & Macmillan

Gill & Macmillan Ltd
Hume Avenue, Park West
Dublin 12
with associated companies throughout the world
www.gillmacmillan.ie
© Gene Kerrigan 2002
0 7171 3459 8
Design and print origination by Carole Lynch
Printed by Omnia Ltd, Glasgow

This book is typeset in Goudy 12 on 16pt.

*The paper used in this book comes from the wood pulp of
managed forests. For every tree felled, at least one tree
is planted, thereby renewing natural resources.*

All rights reserved. No part of this publication may be copied,
reproduced or transmitted in any form or by any means,
without permission of the publishers.

A CIP catalogue record for this book is available
from the British Library.

1 3 5 4 2

For my wife, Julie Lordan

'The President has kept all the promises he intended to keep.'
– *George Stephanopoulos, White House spokesman*

'I don't make jokes. I just watch the government
and report the facts.'
– *Will Rogers*

Contents

1
1. Giving Something Back
How to get started in politics. The money to be
made and the people you have to mix with

47
2. The Economy, Stupid
The low-down on the issue that matters more
than any other

79
3. Climbing the Ladder
The proper way to backstab your colleagues, on the way
to that state car. What to say about tricky issues, while
maintaining an appearance of sincerity

155
4. When the Going Gets Tough
From taking a bribe to giving evidence at a tribunal

1

Giving Something Back

'Politics: The conduct of public affairs for
private advantage.'
– *Ambrose Bierce*

So, You Want to be a Politician

Good for you. Years of sleazy revelations have caused many to see politics as a gathering place for chancers on the make. The best and the brightest turn away from the political arena and choose to make their mark in other fields.

Which is great news. With the softies leaving the field of battle, the way is clear for anyone with the guts to take a few shortcuts to glory. Frankly, the absence of the best and the brightest makes the route to political success – and the considerable goodies attached thereto – that much easier.

To be blunt about it: the scarcity of the finest and the fittest has cluttered up the place with herds of the dull and the dense, many of whom see gormlessness as a state of higher being. It's a wide-open field for those whose ambition is not handicapped by a surplus of scruple. Politics may not pay as well as lawyering, but it's a high-earning business and the path to the top is a damn sight easier, provided you're not more than 15 per cent brain-dead.

So, how do *you* see politics?

Is it a profession? Or a vocation? Do you see the political life as a means of making a good living or do you see it as a calling? Is it a bug that has gripped you? Perhaps you see politics as a game? Or a challenge?

None of these is correct.

Politics is a business.

It is a route to a comfortable living, a degree of status, and a lifetime of free parking in the centre of the capital city.

In today's Ireland, everything is a business. The law is a business, as is medicine, education, the trade in automobiles and the provision of spiritual comfort. If you choose to enter politics, you are selecting a career path on which there are many potholes, but substantial rewards. It pays a lot more than the average wage and the potential perks are limited only by your imagination and your conscience.

The reasons why people are drawn to politics are many and varied. For instance, you may:

(a) have been complaining about the corruption in which public life is steeped, and someone challenged you to do something about it. *Get up off your arse*, they say, *and stand for office and show us all how it's done*. So, you decide, *Damn it, I will*. And off you go, down the yellow brick road towards the Dáil, where you will wise up quickly or be eaten alive;

(b) see politics as an opportunity to reach a position where you can gain influence, and sell it;

(c) be a politics junkie, in which case you will from an early age immerse yourself in constituency statistics, working out the transfers to the 19th decimal point; you will feel driven to shake the hands of thousands of strangers, to make promises you can't possibly keep and to judge every decision on the basis of how it will affect your popularity. This – like a tendency towards country and western music or homosexuality – is a natural condition and there is nothing you can do to change it;

4

(d) want to be famous, and you're no good at football or hurling, and you're too old to join a boy band or a girl band;

(e) have a burning desire for power.

Or, perhaps:

(f) someone in your family died and passed on the safe seat;

(g) you were good at sport, you're bugger all good at anything else and your knees are starting to give out;

(h) you're good at hustling, at making an impression, and there's no other job you're qualified to do that pays nearly as well. (This is the primary reason why a large proportion of career politicians, who haven't a political notion in their heads, get into the politics business.)

If you are successful, eventually someone will ask you why you chose politics as a way of life. You must not, of course, admit to any of the aforesaid motivations. You must say that you feel privileged to live in this great little nation and you wanted to 'give something back'. You 'believe in public service'. The implication must be that you have made a great personal sacrifice in order to serve the public.

Not everyone has the talent necessary to succeed in politics. Steeped in gobdaws it may be, but the politics business requires certain talents and relentless commitment. You must have a single-minded dedication to your own career prospects that not all of us could stomach. You must develop skills not needed in any other human pursuit, not least of which is the ability to instantly switch on an ingratiating smile.

You must be prepared to work long and hard. Never mind the sneers of the media scum: politicians work endless hours and there will be times when you will have to sacrifice your personal comforts. At any time of day or night, a constituent may knock on your door and demand that you do something about some petty problem or other. To others, this person may be a pathetic snivelling gobshite who should be told to bugger off out of it, that you're a legislator, not a fixer. To you, however, this isn't merely a pathetic snivelling gobshite. This is a snivelling gobshite with a vote. You must spend a minimum of four-fifths of your working hours stroking and cuddling such snivelling gobshites, putting them under enough of a compliment to ensure that at the next election they will feel obligated to you.

They will tell their snivelling gobshite relations and friends – if they have any friends – that you are a good man to vote for. The upside to this is that you can consolidate your seat. The downside is that you have opened yourself to a whole new circle of gobshites who will feel free to knock on your door at any time of day or night.

You must cultivate a talent for being able to come down passionately on either side of any argument. Which side you choose depends, obviously, on which side you reckon will come out on top. University debating societies, in which you must learn to argue a case without regard for what you personally believe, are a fine training ground. Some of our most successful lawyers and politicians discovered their natural talents in such academies of two-facedness.

Prepare to dilute your criticism of other politicians. Since general elections these days usually result in coalition, you have to be careful not to grievously offend potential partners. The chancer you slag off today may be an essential hue in tomorrow's rainbow coalition. Buy a thesaurus and lay down a supply of euphemisms. That craw-thumping hypocrite two rows away from you in the Dáil isn't a vicious, small-minded creep – he's a 'colourful' personality. He isn't a sick, cruel, ignorant racist – he has views that are 'debatable'.

Prepare to allow your self-respect to wither. Voters will shake your hand and say something like, 'Begob, you're an honest man, and it's the likes of you we need to put the skids under that crowd of so-called refugees who want to scrounge off our dole, just because a few members of their family were allegedly executed for choosing the wrong side in some so-called civil war or other.'

At that stage, you have to decide if you'll tell him to get stuffed, and watch the votes melt away. Or put on a fixed smile and say something neutral like, 'I take your point.' On the fifteenth occasion you smile weakly at such a smarmy, insufferable moron, you will come to despise yourself with a bitterness that will never die.

If you are not prepared to live with this, in return for a shot at fame and a degree of fortune, find yourself a more congenial business in which to earn a living.

Terms and Conditions

What it lacks in dignity, the politics business makes up in financial reward. In short, few jobs pay this well for the amount of productive work that is required.

The late 1990s' economic boom presented many opportunities for the feathering of various nests. The Dáil was certainly one of them. Your future workplace is fairly bristling with opportunities for the gathering of goodies. As a TD your annual salary is currently €66,000. If you've been in the business for seven years you get a Long Service Increment that brings you up to €68,000; ten years and it's €70,000.

It doesn't stop there.

There are various positions that offer real money. Taoiseach, €126,000; Tánaiste, €99,000; fifteen ministers at €86,000; fifteen junior ministers at €38,000. The Ceann Comhairle gets €86,000, the Leas Ceann Comhairle pulls in €38,000.

Each of these salaries is, of course, on top of the ministers' TD salary of €66,000. Therefore, assuming such officeholders have survived in the Dáil for ten years:

Taoiseach: €196,000

Tánaiste: €169,000

Minister: €156,000

Junior minister:€108,000

(There are also special 'allowances' of €15,000 each for up to two junior ministers who are allowed attend full cabinet meetings. This brings the total salaries of these 'junior-plus' ministers to €123,000.)

That's three dozen deputies, out of 166, earning money on top of their basic TD salary.

In recent years, a number of positions have been created, as part of the reform of the Oireachtas, which present further opportunities for financial enhancement.

There are seven party whips who get between €5,000 and €12,000 each for telling the TDs how to vote.

And each of 20 Oireachtas Committees has to have a chairperson, at around €15,000 a shot. And 18 vice chair-persons, at €8,000. And where you have Oireachtas Committees, you have to have Oireachtas Sub-Committees. And 16 of them have to have chairpersons, at €5,000 a head.

(Oireachtas Committee chairpersons, who get the 'amounts' mentioned above, also get €12,000 'allowances', but this complicates things, so let's not mention it. This is balanced out by the fact that some of the positions have to be allocated to the wasters from the Seanad.)

If you have various committees, you can hardly do without committee 'whips' to keep everyone in line, and they need a stipend of €5,000 per head.

This leaves us with over a hundred positions open to TDs, out of 166, all of which carry handy chunks of cash on top of their TD salaries. (Of course, these rates, which apply at the beginning of 2002, are subject to annual increases.)

It doesn't stop there. Almost half of TDs are also councillors. In an effort to break the 'dual mandate' which allows TDs exercise an effective stranglehold on local democracy, to encourage the growth of a separate local political structure, a payment of around €11,000 a year was agreed in 2001. However, a proposal to end the dual mandate was killed, humiliating the minister – Noel Dempsey – whose cabinet colleagues sold him out after threats from the TD/councillors. The stranglehold was maintained, and the councillors got the increase, anyway. So, for another 80 or so TDs, add an extra €11,000 a year to the income.

It doesn't stop there.

If you live within fifteen miles of Dublin you get €61.53 for each day you clock in to attend the Dáil. This is worth about €5,500 a year. This is on top of your salary; it's just extra money for turning up to do the work you're already paid for.

If you live more than fifteen miles from Dublin there are generous travel and overnight allowances, worth about €12,600 a year. There's a nice little wrinkle to this. Once the Dáil opens for business, even if it knocks off at 2 p.m. and you motor home that afternoon, you can still claim €140 overnight allowance.

And, up to five times a year, you and at least one other TD can 'meet' specially in Leinster House to 'discuss parliamentary business', and claim an overnight allowance, no questions asked. That's another €700 a year, for you and John-Joe 'meeting' to have a few jars in the bar and discuss the latest gossip about who is preparing to knife so-and-so, so that you-know-who's brother-in-law will get the nomination next time.

All this comes with handy pensions attached. You qualify for a TD pension after just three years' service. Likewise for a ministerial pension. Payment of your pension kicks in at 50 years of age, though you can opt for 76 per cent of your pension at 45.

It doesn't stop there.

You also get between €2,740 and €8,780 depending on the size of your constituency, to compensate you for the cost of travelling around saying hello to your constituents, going to funerals, fund-raisers etc. This is tax-free.

If you are a minister, of course, you have the state car and the garda drivers on hand, to take you to the local GAA matches and to bring your missus to the Brown Thomas sales.

You have an office in Leinster House, with the latest computer equipment, but you also need an office in your constituency, perhaps a room in your home, or a room above your brother's pub, so you get an initial €8,800 to buy furniture, office equipment etc (such expenses must be vouched). And then there's another €8,800 a year for the upkeep of that office (no receipts necessary, they'll take your word for this expenditure). And there's another €8,800 a year for secretarial assistance (the spouse or one of the older kids might fill in, here).

It doesn't stop there.

As well as your constituency office you'll need a place to hold your 'clinics', so you get €5,480 a year to rent a room somewhere and to advertise it.

You also, of course, have your office and your secretary at Leinster House, and your free envelopes and free phone and postage there. Plus up to €6,340 a year allowance for your constituency phone bill. You're also provided with a free mobile phone. The bills for this are paid under your phone allowance.

Anyone quibbling about these rates should be informed that politicians' remuneration was set, after much thought, by people who know the value of money, and that pay rises derive from the Programme for Prosperity and Fairness. (Which means, as far as you're concerned, that if you're not prosperous it wouldn't be fair.)

Those are the terms. Now for the conditions.

The Dáil sits for around 90 days a year. This is a little more than half the time the British House of Commons sits. At Christmas, British MPs take three weeks off. That's pagans for you. As practising Christians, we take an unhurried six weeks to pay due respect to the birth of Christ, closing down in mid-December and opening for business at the end of January.

There are the Committees, of course, but these don't require much attention. A handful of overwrought, ambitious TDs use these as platforms from which to gain a higher media profile. If you find that helpful to your career path, by all means feel free to make a fuss. Otherwise, you are sure to be appointed to some committee or other, where you can tag along as a passenger, keeping quiet and picking up some nice loose change if you can snag a whip or a vice-chair position. Probably the most obvious committee passenger in recent years was Denis Foley TD, whose contribution to the Oireachtas Committee investigating tax evasion was less than riveting. As it turned out, Denis knew more about tax evasion than any of his committee colleagues, having a nice little offshore Ansbacher stash of his own.

There are lots of opportunities for international travel. Junkets are arranged to foreign parts, so that TDs and councillors can observe new techniques and procedures in everything from artificial insemination to waste management. The requirements are not oppressive: merely stay upright for part of each day and when reporting back try to remember what country you were in.

There are some drawbacks. In 2001, some TDs visited Argentina and reported back enthusiastically on the lessons we could learn from that country's economic miracle. It was somewhat embarrassing for them when the Argentinean economy collapsed a couple of months later, with riots in the streets. Not to worry, their colleagues wouldn't hold that against them, and there was no question of them losing their places in the queue for the next junket.

You may, if you like, keep your day job. The Dáil workload is not heavy. There simply isn't anything for a TD to do, apart from the odd vote. You don't even have to agonise about how you should vote: the party whip decides that for you. The occasions when you will be required to vote are usually well signposted; otherwise – as a backbencher – you are free to put all your time and energy into getting re-elected. Lots of TDs have found that their public duties have made hardly any impact on their serious work as lawyers, farmers, company directors and such.

If you become a minister you must drop all commercial commitments. In short: simply put everything in the family name and carry on as before, but carefully. (One Fine Gael minister alleged to have continued his involvement in family business had to resign, bitterly protesting his innocence. Another, caught touting for family business, had better connections within the party hierarchy and merely had to move sideways.)

If you're a teacher, get a leave of absence and get some schmuck substitute to fill in for you. You'll be paid the difference between your wages as a teacher and the lesser amount paid to the schmuck substitute. Many TDs and ministers have had their teaching jobs kept open for them for years on end, just in case they needed a fallback position to earn a few bob.

If you want to nail down the Dáil seat and make a lifelong career of it, some application is required. Likewise, if you wish to prosper as a frontbencher. Don't, for instance, get the idea that in the long holiday periods you can simply loll on a beach for weeks on end. The politics business involves long hours and intense work – albeit most of it damn all use to man or beast, involving the running of 'clinics', hand-shaking, funeral-going and the purchase of raffle tickets.

In short, the actual work of a backbench TD hardly

exists: but the work of holding onto the seat is arduous and time-consuming.

However, as you can see, the pay is good and the perks are not to be sneezed at. For instance, get elected just once and you've got free parking for life. As a TD or senator, you may park in Leinster House. When you lose your seat or retire you are entitled to continue using this privilege. If you don't want all the fuss of running for the Dáil and holding onto your seat at one election after another, try the Seanad. Better still, if you have any clout as a business type, see if you can convince a taoiseach to appoint you to the Seanad, thereby avoiding the hassle of an election. Once a member of the Oireachtas, even for the briefest of periods, you've got a free parking space, for life, in the centre of the city. It's worth noting that in August 2001, a 7' x 12' parking space in Dublin city was sold for £45,000. Thankfully, the taxpayers made no big fuss when the parking areas at Leinster House were enlarged in recent years, at great cost to the public purse, to cope with all the accumulated Oireachtas and ex-Oireachtas members now entitled to park there.

If, while gracing the Oireachtas with your presence, you fall into debt, remember that the banks can be very understanding of politicians' problems. The biggie is, of course, Charlie Haughey, who bullied AIB for some years and then had them write off a debt of £400,000. Bear this precedent in mind. Over the years, the banks have written off debts for a variety of politicians, from Fine Gael's Garret FitzGerald (AIB, £180,000 approx.) to Labour's

Dick Spring and a trio of his party hacks (Woodchester, £24,000); from Fine Gael's Bernard Durkan (ACC, £20,000) to Fianna Fáil's John Ellis (NIB, £243,000). The banks, you will find, are understanding of the needs of politicians. And an objective observer might reckon that, through the years, politicians have shown understanding of the needs of banks.

Disclaimer

Distasteful though it may be, it is necessary to pause here and raise an issue that has exercised many of us in recent years. Is honesty all it's cracked up to be?

For decades, the conventional wisdom suggested that whatever faults our politicians might have, financial corruption wasn't one of them. This had nothing to do with piety – it was just that, in a country that never seemed to be over-brimming with excess cash, there didn't appear to be much point to bribing councillors, TDs or ministers. Then, as the economy picked up, from the 1960s onwards, suspicions were voiced about various activities. As we reached the turn of the century, we generated tribunals of inquiry as effortlessly as we spawned expensive coffee houses. As we did a passable imitation of a banana republic *sans* banana trees, it became obvious that corruption had long been as much a part of our political way of life as were funny cardboard hats at election time.

The terms and conditions of the successful politician's employment are such as to make for a comfortable life without the need to stoop to accept bribes. However, your view of the lifestyle to which you wish to become accustomed may suggest that an amount of creative ducking and weaving is indispensable. A number of our best and brightest politicians, as well as some of our worst and thickest, in recent years came to a similar conclusion. Holding a responsible position within the state machine, a person could get fairly comfortable, if not downright rich, if a person was so inclined.

This is entirely your own choice. You may wish to walk the straight and narrow – many politicians do. Or, you may wish to take some shortcuts.

We propose to be non-judgemental about these things, merely pointing out how the world works. Should you choose to make the most of the opportunities presented, that's your business. Some see this as corruption; others see it as enterprise. We live in an entrepreneurial world, where those who are ready to grab the ball and run with it tend to be applauded.

True, there has never been more evidence of political corruption; but, at the same time, has there ever been as much evidence of wealth?

Consider:

Decisions have to be made – for instance – about where houses will be built, about the location and size of shopping centres, the location of factories, the building of roads and other facilities. Those decisions may be made following a certain amount of 'lobbying' by people connected to commercial interests.

It's true that somewhere along the line someone might bung a politician a chunk of money. Is anyone hurt by this?

Well, perhaps. Obviously, such decisions should be made in the interests of efficiency and fairness. To have a housing estate or shopping centre located one place rather than another affects people's lives. To site factories or roads according to the needs of developers rather than citizens is obviously of some significance. It determines who works and who doesn't; whether an area gets a fair share of facilities and prospers, or whether it degenerates. This can determine if people in some part of a city spend half an hour each day stuck in traffic – or an hour and a half. It can be fairly said that while decisions based on 'lobbying' conducted with brown envelopes will enrich developers, notions of fair and efficient planning are destroyed, and the quality of life of thousands can be permanently damaged.

However, without the kind of free market activity that might or might not lead to such occurrences, would we not be a less dynamic, a less entrepreneurial, a less prosperous and a not-so-great little nation?

We draw your attention to the words of Mr Orson Welles, written for his role as Harry Lime in the movie *The Third Man*, and we ask only if this might be the philosophy that has come to dominate Irish politics:

In Italy for thirty years, under the Borgias, they had warfare, terror, murder, bloodshed – but they produced Michelangelo, Leonardo da Vinci and the Renaissance. In Switzerland, they had brotherly love, five hundred years of democracy and peace, and what did that produce . . . the Cuckoo clock?

We make no recommendations or suggestions; we simply outline our understanding of past and current practice.

What is Politics?

Time for some definitions. Politics is, according to the shorter Oxford, 'activities related to pursuit of power, status, etc.' Since this is pretty much the way most of our politicians see things, it is the definition we will accept for the purposes of this guide to political success.

Most politicians and their hangers-on and media groupies define politics as the business of getting elected and staying elected. Which means, it's about constituency profiles and statistics, about first and subsequent preferences, about stroking the voters, watering the grassroots, deals, manoeuvres and back-stabbing; canvassing, polls, promises and getting the vote out on the day.

There is a wider definition of politics. It says that politics involves big issues such as economics and foreign policy. And bigger issues such as jobs and housing, health

40055161

and education, the distribution of resources and all the various decisions that determine how we live. But that need not concern us, such matters being very much secondary to the business of politics in which we hope to succeed, which is: 'activities related to pursuit of power, status, etc.'

What is democracy?

The government of the people, by the people and for the people, and so on.

Who are 'the people'?

Well, now, that's a good question.

There are people who matter; and there are people who don't matter so much. And there are people who hardly matter at all.

The people who matter, the comfortable classes, have clout and money; they have connections. They can have a bearing on how you conduct your business. And you should remain aware of that.

Everyone else – i.e. the rest of 'the people' – can be categorised as 'voters'. Their role in democracy is to vote. In between elections, they may grumble a bit, but by and large they are voters and no more than that.

There is a wider definition of democracy. It says that democracy involves an active citizenry, using access to information, debate and votes, to make choices and ensure efficiency and accountability. And elections are an essential part of that, but only a part.

But that need not concern us, since we are dealing with the business of politics, which is about 'activities related to pursuit of power, status, etc'.

How to Pick a Party to Join

Your first step – unless you have inherited the seat – is to decide what party badge you want to wear. Here is a brief run through the possibilities:

Fianna Fáil: this lot are pragmatic, i.e. they'll say or do whatever it takes to get into power. They have some efficient managers on the team, with not a single principle between the lot of them. Standard 'God Bless the Free Market' policies; used to be in favour of military neutrality but got over it. Utterly shameless.

Fine Gael: they see themselves as 'the good guys', despite having been caught on several occasions accepting sweeties from the usual suspects. Several of them are more likely to be caught reading a book than is the case with the FFers. As a consequence, they look down their noses at their main opponents rather more than is good for them. Unlike FFers, they tend to blush when caught lying or on the take from big business. Standard 'God Bless the Free Market' policies, but not terribly good at implementing them.

Labour: despite having been caught putting the boot just as ruthlessly as the rest of them into the old, the sick and the handicapped, Labour see themselves as pragmatic good guys. Despite a closeness to business interests, they still know how to use radical language and do so without blushing – when in opposition. Used to have a certain degree of internal democracy, but got over it.

Progressive Democrats: these are very principled people, except when their political or personal interests are at stake.

Sinn Féin: we used to think of the Provos as Fianna Fáil with guns. After the ceasefires, they became Fianna Fáil with a lingering nostalgia for things that go bang in the night. Sinn Féin has a number of radical members, with working class roots, but – like Fianna Fáil – they can be expected to get over that.

Ulster Unionist Party: uncompromising unionism.

Democratic Unionist Party: believes the UUP compromises too much.

You could stand as an independent, but that's a tough row to hoe unless you already have deep family or party roots in a constituency. You could start your own party, but that's a large pain. Just thinking of a name presents problems. It has to be positive yet meaningless. The last thing you need is a name that ties you down to a position on the political spectrum. Call yourself the Socialist Party, for instance, or The Greens, and you express a commitment to a position, with the consequence that your appeal is limited to people who agree with you. Even Labour is hampered by a too-explicit name. It remains a minor party, despite decades of demonstrating its willingness to kiss the ass of the wealthy (sorry, that should read: 'to adopt a pragmatic approach to consensus politics').

One of the cleverest party names of modern times was the Progressive Democrats. Two positive words spliced together, it made an instant hit. After all, who doesn't want to be progressive, and who would admit to being anything other than a democrat? Beyond the fact that they couldn't stand Charlie Haughey, it wasn't immediately clear what they stood for, and they soared to around 25 per cent in the polls. Once it became clear that they had explicit rightwing economic policies, linked with liberal social policies, they plunged to 3 or 4 per cent.

Note that Fianna Fáil and Fine Gael prospered for decades using meaningless names, no more than mere tribal howls. What you need is to be meaningless but positive. So, call your new party Forward, for instance, or Onward. Better still, to make the meaning even less clear, give it an Irish name. We suggest Solas, or Suas or Dóchas or Amárach (or even Ámharach) or something like that.

Trouble is, you will eventually have to say something about policies, at which stage you have two options: stand for something or stand for everything. If you genuinely stand for something, you will flop. The political centre is the place to be. From there, by standing for everything, by making your politics as vague as possible, you can seek support from right and left, and prosper. The drawback, however, is that the centre ground is pretty crowded these days.

On the whole, you are better off joining one of the established parties. Which one? There isn't a handspan of difference between the main parties. There is no policy that can't be embraced by any or all of them. Since coalition is probable, and since they'll all climb into bed with just about anyone else, your choice might be determined by your judgement of which will give you the best odds of getting into power.

Fianna Fáil spend more time than anyone else in power. They are the obvious choice. Problem is, everyone knows that, so every chancer with a yen for public office is more likely to choose FF than any other party, making it more difficult to climb through the ranks. With Fine Gael, it's easier to make your mark but you don't spend as much time in government and there are, therefore, fewer opportunities to trade on your position. With Labour, you can – when out of office – throw radical shapes, which is good for the image.

By the way, in case anyone asks: the main difference between Fianna Fáil and Fine Gael is that Fine Gael politicians tend to go to the home of the rich man (John Bruton crawling to Ben Dunne, for instance), to collect a donation. Fianna Fáil politicians have always made a point of maintaining their dignity, having the rich man come to their homes with the brown envelopes (Ben Dunne visiting Charlie Haughey, for instance, or Uncle Tom Cobley visiting Ray Burke).

Since they're all selling the same product, common sense suggests you go with the one displaying the best marketing skills. This was Fianna Fáil, before it got out that the party was getting more backhanders than a New York garbage contractor.

In the end, it comes down to personal preference. Fianna Fáil is for those eager to increase their chances of making money, either legitimately or otherwise, by gaining public office. With Fine Gael you have less chance of getting to shake the money tree, but you get to look down your nose at Fianna Fáil (in between the times when bits of information float to the surface revealing the history of Fine Gael's finances). Labour throws the best parties, so they're the ones to go with if you want to improve your social life. The PDs – well, rumour has it that they hold nice dinner parties.

Getting the Nomination

There are party stars, and there are party gobdaws. You have to decide which you're going to be.

Unless you get a nomination for a Dáil or Council seat, political parties are the last place to be if you want to exercise any political influence. Get a nomination or resign yourself to the fact that your job is to be a fan of the party stars, to stuff envelopes, knock on doors, put up posters and grind your teeth as the party stars betray every principle you thought they stood for.

You get a nomination by making yourself known within

the constituency and making yourself useful within the party. Community groups, charitable and sporting outfits can all be used to get your name known. You must then suck up to the right people within the party. These are people with clout, people with ambitions. An example of such ambitions might be an appointment to a board of some kind; or political support for certain business projects. Discuss these things frankly and make the necessary promises in return for their backing.

Who are your main enemies in trying to win a seat?

No, not the candidates from the opposing parties. They'll win the votes of their own party's supporters and a bigger or larger share of the floating vote, depending on how well they campaign. Your main enemies are the other candidates from your own party.

All of you will be primarily competing for your party's core vote. You will need to take a large percentage of that vote. Only if you do so does it matter a damn how much of the floating vote you win in competition with the shower from the other parties. Against candidates from the other parties you must be tough; against ambitious individuals from your own party you must be ruthless.

Make alliances with others to do down your mutual enemies. Your allies will help you undermine those who stand in your way, in return for your help in undermining those they wish to shaft.

It helps if, from early on, you quietly promote the nomination of weak candidates to run with you. Make friends with the weak, conspire with them to undermine stronger would-be candidates. When it comes time to screw them, they'll be open, trusting and vulnerable.

You and your party colleagues may divide the constituency up between you and each look for first preferences within your own area. This is sensible. It's known as vote management, and it aims to maximise the party vote. However, your constituency colleagues will invariably break this agreement and poach votes in your area. The only sensible thing to do is stab them in the back first, by campaigning ruthlessly for first preferences in every part of the constituency you can reach.

They will complain about you to the party bosses. So, you should get your complaints in first, even before they break the agreement. That way, when they complain about you, you can reply angrily that you are merely defending yourself by responding in kind to their treachery.

Which political arena should you aim for?

There's good money in the EU. However, the MEP positions are well sewn up by party hacks and has-beens. You'd want to be well in for a few years before you'd have a shot at one of them.

As an up-and-coming politician, you might find that a senate seat can be a handy launch pad to the Dáil. Otherwise, it's bugger all use. Mostly it's a haven for failed TDs, or those politicians too old for anything else but not quite ready to bow off the public stage. The senate, having no power, is mainly useful to blow-hards who fancy themselves as orators but haven't the stomach for the tough route to a Dáil seat. In the senate, they can spray the air with their unfunny wit and their clichéd opinions: rolling up their sleeves and putting their noses to the grindstone, while simultaneously pulling up their socks, grabbing the dilemma by the horns and riding their hobbyhorses until the cows come home to roost. Strictly for losers.

If you think you're ministerial material, the Dáil should be your target. As a minister, the opportunities for advancement and enrichment are many and various. Otherwise, go for the council, where there are lucrative possibilities. Mere backbench TDs are damn all use to anyone; councillors have some power over decisions involving land and property. At €11,000 a year, the pay isn't bad for a part-time job. Unless you become a pivotal figure on the council, the perks and the occasional bribes are usually small but the opportunities are many. It all adds up.

The local council is a fine base from which to launch a Dáil career. Once you get into the Dáil, the council seat is invaluable for protecting your base and stifling potential competition from up-and-coming hustlers. TDs hanging onto their council seats have effectively killed local democracy: a small price to pay for enhanced security of tenure for our national legislators.

Often, an enthusiastic newcomer is offered a hopeless nomination, for an unwinnable seat, where the veterans have all the seats sewn up. Hardened hacks refuse the honour, because their egos can't face the prospect of an arduous campaign and certain failure. If you get a chance, take such an offer. The function of a no-hope candidate is to soak up the party's support in geographical areas where the main candidate is weak, and pass on the second preferences to the candidate who matters. Without such a no-hope candidate, votes would drift away to other parties.

Running as a certain loser is disheartening. But you have shown your loyalty; they owe you a favour. Should the main candidate fall under a bus, or is caught with an offshore tax hidey-hole, a swift resignation may be on the cards. It is possible that he or she may become the victim of dreadfully unfair but accurate rumours involving someone else's spouse, offspring or family pet. Suddenly, the party will be looking around for a loyal campaigner with a spotless record and some experience of campaigning.

Of course, it's important that the rumours are not traceable.

Theory and Practice

Here's the score: as a politician, you are on a career path. When you stand in a general election you are one of less than 500 candidates for 166 positions. The odds are not that bad, about one chance in three, which is better odds than you'll get in applying for any other job where the terms, pay and conditions are as good.

Many candidates are fools or cranks, running for the exercise; many are principled people who want to help make the world a better place – i.e. born losers. So, we can dismiss at least a third of the candidates, who will lose their deposits. That leaves about 300 running for 166 seats.

Among this 300 or so are a little more than 100 TDs who are going to retain their seats. They are career politicians who have the skills to hold onto their seats as long as they want to – and who have browbeaten, blackmailed, out-manoeuvred or bribed anyone likely to be any kind of a threat. It takes two or three elections before the seat is secure; some never manage the trick.

So, that leaves 200 or so other candidates, fighting for around 50 seats.

Of those 50 seats, about ten will be earmarked for former TDs re-taking seats from which they were ejected. Another ten or so will be taken by senators, moochers who have used the Seanad to build a base from which to run. That leaves in and around thirty seats that are truly up for grabs. About thirty TDs currently sitting in those seats will get their P45s; thirty new TDs will arrive.

If you've done your homework and identified the vulnerable seats – and this might well determine which party you decide to join – you can work out your chances of being one of those thirty.

Before going any further, it is necessary to say something about what we might call *The Theory and Practice of Politics*.

We live in a parliamentary democracy, and there's much to be said for that. Parliamentary democracy is an advance on much that has gone before; for instance, it beats feudalism and totalitarianism hands down. It fends off those blank-eyed chaps who believe that there isn't a social or political problem that can't be solved with either a blast from an AK47 or the sizzle from a carefully placed set of electrodes.

What is parliamentary democracy?

The Oireachtas is a body where all the varied – sometimes conflicting – interests in the state are brought together. We do this by electing Dáil deputies to represent our interests. They embody the interests of farmers and factory workers, urban and rural, business and unions, rich and poor, the privet-trimmed gentility of suburbia and the graffiti-ridden inner city. In parliament, the representatives of these forces debate the issues of the day and arrive at a workable compromise. Taking its brief from this debate, Cabinet constructs the laws and regulations necessary to ensure prosperity, fairness and justice for all.

That's the theory.

Here's the practice.

The Cabinet, appointed by the taoiseach alone, manages the affairs of the state. It draws up laws and regulations in consultation with the civil service, having consulted lobbyists for the interests on which party funding and support are dependent.

End of story.

Only in the most exceptional circumstances does the Dáil or Seanad have any function other than to pass everything through on the nod, the politicians voting in accordance with instructions from the party whips.

Politicians are told at parliamentary party meetings about the legislation coming up; they may quibble a bit about it, but mostly they know so little about the detail and effects of the legislation that is being put before them that they might as well be looking into a bush. The function of a parliamentary party meeting is not to consider the direction in which the nation is to be steered. It is to ensure that impending legislation contains no little wrinkles that might affect the party's electoral prospects. And to ensure that any quibbles anyone might have are flushed out and disposed of behind closed doors and not in parliament.

When a piece of legislation might threaten the interests of a sizeable number of their constituents, individual TDs are allowed kick up a bit of a fuss. They may even, in extreme cases, vote against such legislation and be suspended from the party. Should you ever be in this position, don't worry about it. This is all done with nods and winks; it allows the legislation through, while boosting the TD's image as someone who can be relied on by the voters. The TD is always quietly accepted back into the fold in time for the next election.

Every four or five years, voters get to make some marks on a sheet of paper. This is the extent of their involvement in democracy. A huge array of public relations outfits, including your little constituency machine, lays into them as they decide what marks to make. They might vote for you because you're the party candidate and their family traditionally votes that way; or because you shook hands with them once outside a shopping centre; or because they liked what your leader said on TV last week; or because of some stand the party took two years back; or because another party irritates them; or because you look cute and convincing.

Whatever the reason, once they vote your party into power it can claim to have a mandate to implement its election programme. The voters won't have heard of at least 90 per cent of these policies; they won't have had enough information to understand the implications of most of the rest, but the party can still claim to have a mandate for it all. (See *How to Launch an Election Manifesto*.)

In between elections, the government is subject to pressure from various forces. These may be chambers of commerce; cartels; professional bodies; trade unions; tenant and community groups; single-issue campaigns. All seek to enhance their position relative to everyone else. Much of this is done openly, in social conflict, involving strikes, picketing, publicity campaigns. Some of it – involving circles, golden or otherwise – is done quietly. Money changes hands, favours are called in, people look after one another.

In short, you'll find that the voters are one constituency that must be kept sweet; but they are just one of several, some of which exert far stronger, inexorable, pressures.

How to Shake Hands

Today, most politicians operate within a very narrow political spectrum; they all say more or less the same thing about everything. Image counts far more than content. Therefore, your main political focus must be not on what you say but on how you say it.

Remember: the majority of votes in your constituency will already be sewn up, through party loyalty or habit, through favours done or bribes given. The floating vote decides where the seat goes. Floating voters can be discerning types, choosing carefully where their precious vote should go. More often, they are gormless gobdaws who have never given serious matters a moment's thought and are influenced primarily by image. Your job is to create an image that will win the loyalty of the gobdaws, without saying or doing anything that will alienate the voters already sewn up.

Shake a lot of hands. Travel around your constituency as much as possible. Never mind the cynics, voters love meeting politicians. In meeting the punters, your job is to invest a short, meaningless encounter with some significance. If the local hurling team has recently won a match, refer to it. Perhaps you're canvassing at a newsagent's where someone is filling in a Lotto coupon – smile and say, 'Begod, I hope you picked the right numbers, there, so I do!'

Now, some people might smile tolerantly at this, while inside they're thinking: 'What a sad lot these politicians are, hustling without shame.' Screw them. Their minds are probably made up, anyway.

There are many simple, undemanding people in this great little nation. Their interest in your fate is shallow. They are allowed hardly any influence on the forces that shape their lives. Every four years or so they are allowed put some marks on a piece of paper. Their political reflection consists solely of deciding where to make those marks. And a personal encounter with a politician is something they will remember. With this effortless but powerful interaction, you have made yourself larger than life to such punters. Next time, faced with a choice between you and someone who remains just a face on a poster, they'll vote for you. And they'll tell their friends you're a decent sort.

It is amazing how effective a handshake and a few personal words can be. Since political parties today are motivated by little other than their own need to get into power, many rank and file political party activists are apolitical. They are fiercely loyal to one party or another, as a fan is loyal to a football club; but a truly political thought has never cast a shadow across their unruffled minds. Some are busybodies, who like to imagine they are busily engaged in the work of the nation; many just want to rub shoulders with councillors, TDs, and ministers. *And here is the most important lesson you can possibly learn in Irish politics: remember names.* To meet someone again a year later, and to remember his or her name, has an astonishing effect. They will see themselves as having been noticed and singled out as special, and they will work their arses off to get you re-elected.

Train your memory. As a backup, a trusted local party activist should be assigned the job of prompting you with names, as casually as possible. As you're shaking hands with one gobdaw, you're listening as your crony calls out to an approaching party minnow: 'Come over here, Séamus, and shake hands with the man himself.'

'Begod', says you, turning to greet the mug as though the purpose of your visit has finally been fulfilled, 'Séamus, you're looking well.'

Shake hands firmly. The grip is important. Hold the mug's hand and simultaneously grasp his elbow with your free hand. Shake the hand vigorously, like you're pumping water from a well; hold onto his hand a few seconds more than is necessary, as though you are reluctant to let go, but you have a schedule to keep. If possible, throw in some detail from your last meeting. 'Begod, Séamus, I take it you didn't win the Lotto that time, what?!' Laugh, pat Séamus on the shoulder. This is important. People like to be touched by the people they admire. Someone stops you on the street: as you talk, you should – as though unconsciously – reach out and touch their forearm. That kind of thing establishes bonds. (Needless to say, this must not be overdone, or someone is bound to start rumours about how you can't keep your hands to yourself.)

Establish 'clinics', to which voters will come in the hope of a political cure for whatever ails them. Tiresome as these places are, they are wonderful for putting people under a compliment to you.

Find out as much routine detail as you can about the local busybodies, the big fish in the small ponds, the local party gobdaws. You can then casually inquire of some party hack as to how his young fella is doing in UCD, or if the ma is over the operation yet. That kind of thing ties them tightly to you.

Buy raffle tickets for charities and community causes. Attend funerals; people are impressed that you take time off your busy schedule to pay your respects.

Establish touts on the local council to keep you informed of who is about to get a grant of some sort, a pension or an allowance; write to them, congratulating them. They will always associate your name with good news. With luck, they'll think you had something to do with arranging it.

Finally, on voting day, get on the road, constantly travelling from one polling station to another. Shake hands until your hand is raw. Lots of people turn up to vote not out of conviction but because they are convinced they have a duty to do so. They believe that if they don't vote for someone – anyone – they are somehow betraying the heroes who fought to make old Ireland free. Smile at voters, wink, joke and simper. A surprising number of voters arrive at polling stations still only loosely committed to any candidate, or even totally uncommitted. There is a reasonable chance that your last-minute handshake will swing them. Your handshakes might influence just one in a hundred. And one voter in a hundred adds up to a one per cent swing. And that can win or lose a seat.

How to Count Votes

Here we come to the importance of what we might call Amateur Cute Hoors. (We will deal, by and by, with the importance of the Professional Cute Hoor.)

The qualification for an Amateur Cute Hoor is an ability to use a pencil to make a mark. You sit one of these individuals at each box in the polling station, with a copy of the relevant pages from the electoral register. If you don't have enough of these cute hoors to go around, you can usually arrange with other candidates to share the burden, as it is in your mutual interest to cooperate.

Each voter coming to collect a ballot paper must give a name; your cute hoor marks that name off the list. In theory, your cute hoor is there to prevent personation. In practice, when the polling is over you have a list of every-one who voted in each individual box. And each box is identified by number.

Next day, at the count centre, you station your cute hoors along the rails, as the boxes are opened, one by one, and the votes counted. Your cute hoors mark, on specially prepared lists, the number on the side of the box and a tally of the numbers of first preferences each candidate gets from that box. Some cute hoors are smart enough to be able to get down a fair amount of information about second and even third preferences. These are the 'Tallymen', beloved of media legend.

While the election officials are counting the total votes for each candidate, from all the boxes together, you now have:

- a list of everyone who voted in a particular box, with his or her address
- a list of precisely how the first preferences were cast within that box.

The constituency party, if it is any use, will have detailed records of the results of canvasses in each street. From these, and from local knowledge, it is possible – to a useful extent – to crack the secrecy of the ballot box. Knowing precisely where the party's strengths and weaknesses are allows you to work on them for future elections. It gives you a crucial edge over the amateurs who, every now and then, imagine they can break into politics just because they stand for something or other. As a political pro, you will recognise that such idealism leads only to anarchy.

Gifted amateurs, and those who coast along on dissent, can occasionally beat the system and get elected. Changes in constituency boundaries and the fluctuations of party image at national level can affect an outcome. Mostly, however, the kind of information you have gathered can be used for decades to maintain a grip on a constituency.

There are plans, by busybody reformists, to bring in electronic voting, which will badly damage this set-up. However, the process is at an experimental stage. It will take years to develop, and if we put on enough pressure – for instance, by complaining that this soulless technology will put an end to the Tallyman, a quaint and harmless part of our democratic tradition – we can slow it to a crawl, if not stop it altogether.

(By the way, the practice of having cute hoors collect the names of those who vote won't be stopped. And, having mentioned personation, it may occur to you that having lists of all those who voted, election after election, might also provide you with a list of those who never bother to vote. And that this might be useful to anyone who wanted to organise a bunch of corner boys to turn up and use the names of the non-voters, or those who died since the list was last revised, in order to illegally influence the outcome of the election. Needless to say, we don't recommend this course. Unless the margins are tight and you're desperate.)

Know Your Colleagues

When you make it into the Dáil you will be one of 166 Deputies. Pretty tough odds against making it into the Cabinet, you might think. Not so. The hard work has been done.

Of this 166, approximately 70 will have the IQ of a turf briquette. This is not an insult; it is an observable fact. The system of election encourages the success of cunning hoors and ruthless simpletons. It is a fact that the percentage of spoiled votes in Seanad elections, in which the electorate consists mostly of professional politicians, is twice the percentage of spoiled votes in a general election. In short, the average politician is twice as likely to make a pig's mickey of filling in a simple ballot paper as is the average citizen. These are people who move their lips when they think. Ten minutes after being elected, they begin preparing for the next election; and this goes on through their lives, decade after decade, until they drop dead or retire. These people see no other purpose in life but to be elected and re-elected. They have a deep, burning personal need to be elected. They are single-minded and cold-blooded about it, relentless in their pursuit of 'the seat'. The Dáil has no meaning for them other than as a base from which to be re-elected next time. They know nothing at all about the legislation they vote through; they spend hardly any time in the Dáil chamber; yet they work 80 hours a week, ceaselessly stroking their constituents.

These cretins are ruthless in their opposition to a functioning local democracy and a system of efficiently vetting claims for state benefits; they want to keep their own sweaty little hands on the levers of patronage. They agree with French poet Paul Valéry, that 'politics is the art of preventing people from taking part in affairs that properly concern them.' A large proportion of TDs are also local councillors. They effectively privatise whole areas of public administration, for their own electoral advantage. At their 'clinics', they collect the raw material of their political lives: the personal problems, needs and hopes of the voters. They never tell anyone straight out – 'Sorry, you're not entitled to that.' When people are not getting some benefit to which they are entitled, the TDs don't seek to organise communities or sectors that are unfairly deprived or in need: they don't seek to politically redress a wrong. They prefer to make individuals beholden to them.

They write letters to ministers and departments; they make phone calls, hounding civil servants. They don't direct constituents to the appropriate state agency for dealing with their problems; they promise to 'put a word in', then they hassle civil servants. They use those problems as ropes of loyalty to bind the voters to them.

Anybody questioning this state of affairs you should dismiss with the remark that politicians 'deal with the real needs of real people'.

The most effective word in your armoury is 'real'. You deal with 'real' people. In a 'real' way. Unlike leftwing pinko critics, who live in an airy-fairy utopia. You live in the 'real' world.

As noted, the Dáil sits for around 90 days a year. Three months off in the summer, six weeks at Christmas. Don't think, however, that this means you can spend weeks on end in Lanzarote, with a knotted hanky on your head. TDs spend little time on Dáil business because that's not where their main work is. Their main work is in the constituencies, campaigning for the next election.

It takes up a lot of time to attend funerals and football and hurling matches, and to buy raffle tickets. They buy drinks and recommend people for jobs for which they are not remotely qualified; they invite constituents to the Dáil and get them drunk in bars in the vicinity of Leinster House; they arrange for deputations to meet ministers; they plead with the Minister for Justice for convictions to be quashed. They have excellent secretarial back-up, and free postage, so they can remind constituents of all the favours they've done for them. It never occurs to them to research political problems and contribute to or initiate legislation. Why legislate for people's needs when you can get them to queue up to ask you to do them a favour? Anyway, what has legislation got to do with politics?

Legislation is drawn up at cabinet level; the party TDs have a chance to say something about it at parliamentary party meetings, but few bother. Cunning hoors and ruthless simpletons have no views on anything coming before the Dáil unless it is the kind of Bill that stirs up controversy among their constituents. In that case, it might have an influence on their chance of being re-elected. They will, therefore, take a strong stand, threatening to bring down the government if the legislation is not dropped. Since the party leaders are aware of this, such legislation is usually shown quietly to a number of the most backward politicians in the House. If it's not okay with them, it's quietly smothered.

The party whips tell the TDs when and how to vote in the Dáil, and the cunning hoors and ruthless simpletons do so cheerfully, never reading the Bills they are bringing into law. They spend their entire working lives at this kind of thing, paying little attention to politics. They genuinely believe that this *is* politics. The major political events and developments of their times will pass them by, of interest only if they threaten to cause an election.

About 60 more Deputies will have average brainpower,

but no ministerial ambition whatever. Many of them are decent, modest sorts who drifted into politics for vague reasons: because they were good at getting elected; or they couldn't think of anything else to do; or they had some notion of serving the public interest. They occasionally make articulate speeches; some of the better ones will openly and seriously question party policy perhaps two or three times in an entire working life. The thought of being appointed minister might once have crossed their minds and caused a small gush of saliva – the state car is handy, the money is great, the prestige is mighty and the patronage and the goodies available for distribution in the constituency can practically nail the seat to your arse for life. But, for these people, the thought of making decisions with consequences, standing up where your enemies and the media scum can take endless pot-shots, is too frightening.

That leaves about three-dozen serious contenders for ministerial office. At any one time, about half of the three dozen will be in opposition. That leaves about 18 capable contenders for the 30 positions available – 15 cabinet positions, and 15 positions as mini-minister. When the party achieves power, these 18 will be appointed, with another dozen gobdaws making up the numbers.

So, once you become a TD, and you've figured out which asses to kiss, you're ambitious, presentable and articulate, you appear to have more than half a brain and you're sober at least three days out of seven, the chances of being appointed to office are very good indeed.

If you are to be a cabinet minister, it is necessary for you to have some understanding of the subject that matters more than any other to the voters.

2

The Economy, Stupid

'I've been rich and I've been poor. Rich is better.'
– *Sophie Tucker*

This Great Little Nation

Once upon a time, it was easy being an Irish politician. All you had to do was let an occasional howl out of you. Something to do with getting the Brits out of the Fourth Green Field would do. Or how the young people were letting us all down by not speaking the First Official Language. Or how television would land us all in Hell, so it would. Or how the communists would turn us all into Russians if we didn't drive them out of the trade unions.

At election time, you might well get up on the back of a lorry and demand, at the top of your voice, that the Pope's latest encyclical should be translated into the First Official Language and the Irish air force should drop thousands of copies on the young people of Belfast, to encourage them to smash their TV sets over the heads of the nearest communist trade unionist and rise up and drive the Brits out.

In short, it was a simpler time. In other countries, governments rose and fell on their competence in dealing with the economy. Here, we didn't need an economy; we had emigration.

After independence, we were so pleased with ourselves for having kicked out the Brits that it was a while before we noticed that, having taken over the country, we now had the job of running it. And that involved a little more than deciding which party hacks should be appointed subpost master of every village and town in the land.

So, for the want of something better to do, we had an economic war with the Brits, but that didn't last too long. After that, we kind of hunkered down and made a virtue of our economic stagnancy. To be frugal was to be holy. Nutrition merely made young people soft. True Christians would have no truck with school heating that worked, homes with indoor toilets and the like. We were an oasis of spiritual success in a world of pagan materialism.

The sons and even the occasional daughter of the comfortable classes filled the available spaces in higher education; those who didn't gravitate to the civil service and the professions inherited daddy's small business. The economy chugged on, generating just enough heat to warm the backsides of the comfortable classes. This required some tens of thousands of people each year to bugger off out of it on the emigrant ships and seek succour from the pagan Brits.

From the mid-1960s, a somewhat more adventurous crew took over. They were what we might call the Haughey generation. Their traditional nationalism was tempered by a love for the lifestyle that modern Europe had to offer. These chaps didn't see much of a future in frugality.

What to do? They noticed that most of Europe was experiencing a long post-war boom, driven by increased trade. They noticed that only the dictatorships of Spain and Portugal (two more good Catholic countries) shared Ireland's policy of national self-sufficiency. And both of them were as economically and socially stagnant as we were. So, with the help of some open-minded civil servants, the Haughey generation of politicians decided the future lay in opening the economy to international capital.

The economy grew. The country opened up socially, emerging from decades of inwardness. There were ups and downs, short booms and long recessions. A number of people became very rich, not all of them by dubious means. But it was pretty thin gruel, and the waves of emigrants continued to bugger off out of it. And by the 1980s the frustration was such that the politicians decided their economic objectives could be met by the simple strategy of borrowing. When the bills came due, it was merely a matter of squeezing the hospitals and the schools.

As ever, there were ways of easing the strain. Obliging developers, hotel owners and supermarket tycoons were so admiring of major politicians that they showered them with money. Whether you were a proud taoiseach or a humble councillor, there was usually someone willing to see you right. And if political decisions made those people even richer, wasn't that just the way of things?

Leading business figures made their own arrangements to ease the tax burden, via offshore accounts operated by enterprising accountants. Tens of thousands of owners of small businesses made imaginative if unlawful arrangements with the banks.

(You'll find that, from time to time, this history of alleged corruption is thrown up in your face, with insinuations that you're all at it. The best response to this is a dignified statement that such things happened long,

long ago, and were greatly exaggerated by leftwing pinko politically correct types. And, anyway, nothing of that sort could happen today.)

Then, in the mid-1990s, after over twenty years membership of the EU, the Irish economy finally caught up with the rest of Europe; it clicked into place, and that place was as a piece of the Euro jigsaw, with connections into the global economy through servicing the foreign investment strategy of US companies.

Nowadays, it isn't so easy to be an Irish politician. Letting a howl out of you about the Fourth Green Field will get you nothing more than some puzzled glances and a Special Branch tap on your phone. Today, what matters to the comfortable classes who will constitute the greater part of the constituency that you must stroke is the economy and what it can do for them. Will it allow them climb the property ladder? Will it allow them replace their car with this year's model before the end of January? Can they aspire to Armani proper, or must they slum it with Emporio Armani? Will they be able to maintain their latte lifestyle? Is a Louis Vuitton handbag out of the question?

There's nothing to be gained by mentioning that most of what happens to the economy is beyond the powers of politicians. To succeed in Irish politics today, you will need a plausible-sounding economic theory about how you propose to maintain and improve the lifestyle of ever-larger numbers of class-conscious (in every sense of the term) voters. Otherwise, they'll get very grumpy.

We cannot tell you, as an aspiring politician, what to do about the economy. We can only advise you on what to say.

How to Explain a Boom

If someone asks you why the Irish economy began booming in the mid-1990s, achieving growth rates that other countries couldn't imagine in their wettest of fiscal dreams, here's what to say.

Well, you see, it was like this:

From 1987, a very few farsighted and courageous politicians set out to free the Irish economy from the shackles of high public spending, high taxes, ever-increasing budget deficits, low morale and high unemployment. They were aided in this by a very few farsighted and courageous public servants who broke free from the plodding, backward, cautious, public service mentality. Let us not forget the role of the 'social partners', who put aside their sectional interests, ended the class war and – instead of each of them fighting for a bigger slice of the cake – cooperated in making the cake bigger for everyone. Shoulder to shoulder with these pioneers, stood a very few farsighted and courageous business innovators who put their cutting-edge imaginations to work and took chances that paid off, smashing the inferiority complex that chained the hostage of business culture to the radiator of the nanny state.

The example set by these brash, serious-but-fun-loving entrepreneurs was picked up by a new generation of well-educated young people, imbued to the marrow with faith in the logic, efficacy and fairness of the Free Market. This new generation spilled forth from the colleges and universities – where the farsighted and courageous politicians had put in place a state-of-the-art education system – eager to 'throw off the shackles' of caution, to 'pick up the ball' and to 'run with it'. Result: the Celtic Tiger, a tough, street-smart and wholly new species of kick-ass economy, making us the envy of Europe.

Christ! They were coming here from all over the goddamn world to see how we did it!

And – do you know what? – we managed to do it without losing our essential Irish charm.

We remained as fresh and culturally vibrant a nation as we had always been. We ended up not alone 'creating a new economic paradigm' – to which all the old rules didn't apply – we also remained just as cute as ever.

We were now *a tiger*, damn it – and that excused some of the hard-nosed brutalism that was a necessary consequence of our uninhibited commitment to market forces. But we were a *Celtic* tiger, so we remained lovable.

That's the way to tell the story. You must keep a straight face as you do it.

Things You Mustn't Say

The problem with this story is that you have to tell it with a fresh-faced enthusiasm usually found only among newly self-aware young folk who have recently discovered sex. While they know that previous generations cannot have been wholly celibate, they firmly believe that no one has ever done the business with the energy, skill, enthusiasm and imagination they bring to the task.

Such confidence among teenagers is endearing; the naïvety of adults throwing teenage shapes is less so.

When telling this story there are things you mustn't say. First off: you may mention the US boom, but try to make it sound like a spin-off from our own. Try to avoid placing the Irish boom in the context of global developments.

For a decade, the US economy boomed relentlessly; huge amounts of jobs were created – not all of them requiring the workers to wear a polyester uniform and urge their customers to have a nice day. Unlike his predecessor, President Clinton didn't have to worry about a declining economy. This left him enough free time to play peacemaker on the world stage. And to accept more than garlic bread as a side order when Monica Lewinsky delivered his pizza.

The US boom was in turn part of the global economy, which was going through a wild ride of its own. One big market, gigantic corporations with economies bigger than some countries, marketing on a world-wide scale; computers speeding everything up, transferring money, stocks and shares around the globe in microseconds, instant sales and purchases of goods not yet manufactured, as hordes of savvy young gamblers jabbed at their computer screens and screamed into their telephone headsets, speculating, boosting, undermining, making a killing.

As the potential of new technology – computers, mobile phones, the internet – fed hopes and greed, larger numbers of gamblers were drawn into a shared marketplace. Hardened speculators and wizened old fund managers now competed with certifiable headbangers. There arose the phenomenon of 'day traders', for instance, losers who drooled over their home computers, a spreadsheet in one hand, a copy of the *Wall Street Journal* in the other, analysing company performance and share movements, dipping in and out of the market, possessed of an insane belief in their own cunning.

Once upon a time, fools like that would just withdraw their savings, cash in their insurance policies, and head for Las Vegas for the weekend, where they'd blow it all at the poker tables, destroying their lives and the lives of those who loved them. The odd fool would be found, on a Monday morning, somewhere out in the desert, a gun in his mouth and what little brains he used to have spread all over the inside of his hired car. Now, such fools chose instead to gamble on the Free Market, operating from a spare bedroom converted into a 'profit centre', slack-jawed in front of a PC screen as their dreams evaporated. Occasionally one of them turned up at a broker's office some Monday morning, feeling aggrieved, bristling with the weaponry he was constitutionally entitled to bear, and he'd shoot four or five people before the local constabulary blew what little brains he used to have straight out of his skull.

Such fools were no longer merely trashing the family savings, they – along with the dotcom kids, the conmen and the market pundits, the panicky fund managers, the cool sharks, the politicians, the consultants, the always-optimistic market analysts, the media and the would-be investment advisors who were trying for the big time with someone else's money – were collectively playing games with the global economy. They were part of the bullish mood that Alan Greenspan, chairman of the Federal Reserve, described as 'irrational exuberance'.

And that bullish mood was felt as strongly in the wine bars and coffee emporia of Dublin as in the most optimistic heights of Wall Street.

Don't mention any of this when you're explaining how the Irish geniuses figured out how to turbo-charge the domestic economy.

US companies were investing overseas; they wanted a foothold in the EU market, and where better than in good old Ireland. After years of high unemployment and 'social partnership', the trade unions were house-trained. As a nation, we were deferential to outsiders who promised investment; we had low corporate taxes; we spoke English; we had hordes of IDA chappies trained to bow and scrape and act as agents for outsiders bearing jobs. We had an education system that had been quite deliberately and thoroughly adjusted to the needs of business.

A survey of 2,958 businesses, conducted by academics at the University of Maastricht, sought to discover the effective corporate tax rate – that is, the real tax rate when all accounting differences are calculated – across Europe. We shouldn't mention it, but the Irish rate was half the EU average.

Don't mention the transfer pricing scam. Multinational firms that make profits elsewhere manipulate internal pricing, artificially reducing the profits made in other countries, and pretending those profits were made in low-corporate-tax-Ireland: this boosts the apparent productivity of the Irish economy. One effect of this is that we've not been entirely sure of the accuracy of our economic statistics. When we have evidence of high exports in a sector, is it real or have a percentage of the goods been manufactured elsewhere, 'bought' by one arm of a multinational and imported here, to be wrapped and 'exported' again, claiming the bulk of the profits were made here, and so availing of our low tax? To put it another way, what percentage of the goods said to be manufactured and exported here consists of nothing more than the plastic wrapper that we put on the goods?

And here's the bit you really mustn't mention: all along, we provided cheap labour.

Even by the turn of the century, after years of productivity going through the roof, while we strutted and preened and boasted about how our natural superiority had transformed the economy, we were just plain cheap to employ. Hourly labour costs in Ireland were only 73 per cent of the EU average. Only Portugal, Greece and Spain had lower rates.

Another thing we try not to bring up is the role of the European Union. You may, in passing, dismissively allow that we got some 'transfers' from the EU. Don't mention the three billion per year in solid cash that went into infrastructure, training and education.

Reality, in one paragraph:

An economically backward country was – with the help of massive transfers from the EU – brought close to the European norm, at a time when the US economy was enjoying a prolonged boom and manoeuvring to take advantage of the single European market. Ireland was available and accommodating. Result: an unprecedented period of growth that was driven by global forces more than by any tigerish behaviour of our own. We did what the Dutch and the Belgians and the Norwegians and the Danes did, what every modern economy does when it gets the chance: with the instincts, energy and wit that is native to humans – and not just to the cool Irish – we took advantage of a fortunate turn of events. And fair play to us.

But don't mention any of that.

And play this down: as the economy stirred, as confidence rose, the moneylenders went to work, pushing credit at goggle-eyed customers like ecstasy dealers at a rave. And like lit-up, switched-on dancers, we took what we were offered, by the bucket-load. The credit flowed into personal consumption, into share speculation and to fund new businesses. Sometimes those businesses were firmly based, often they were for the birds: it didn't matter – grab the credit, get in on the boom, get a taste of that ecstasy and go back for more.

What Happened to the Boom?

It was the foot and mouth that did it, for starters. Then a bunch of mad Arabs carried out a series of atrocities on 11 September 2001, and the consequences were hugely damaging to the world economy, severely damaging the wonderful achievements of our entrepreneurial classes, but that was just a temporary setback, because the economy's fundamentals remained sound.

That's the story you stick with. In truth, the US boom had come to an end months earlier and the consequences were already being felt over here. The insanity of the dotcom bubble had been pricked. Thankfully, there was a silver lining to the cloud of dust that hung over Manhattan on 11 September. The shadows from that cloud came in handy for hiding certain realities, of which there is now no need at all to remind the punters.

If anyone asks how come people were queuing up to take credit for the boom, but the same geniuses neither predicted, explained nor took responsibility for the downturn, tell them to grow up. If anyone points out that the economy was already in trouble when the Arabs struck, tell them they are being unpatriotic, undermining national confidence. If they persist, accuse them of giving aid and comfort to terrorists, not to mention displaying despicable anti-Americanism. That last bit makes no sense, but no matter: it always shuts them up.

Above all, it is important to stress that downturns are temporary, while the great leap forward of the New Ireland is permanent. It is important, for the sake of national morale, that we keep the focus on the triumphs of the entrepreneurs.

Don't Mention the Recession

As a politician, you will be sought out by the media and asked for your views on the state of the economy. You should bear in mind Gore Vidal's dictum: 'Never turn down an opportunity for sex, or to appear on television.'

When speaking on the economy, there is a golden rule: in uncertain times, you may say 'downturn' or 'dip', but you mustn't say 'recession'. Saying 'recession' is almost as bad as saying 'slump', which is pretty close to saying 'depression' and rather than say 'depression' you should bite your tongue off and bury it at low tide.

There is a cycle: boom is followed by downturn, then recession, a shakeout of the weakest, growth of the strongest, leading to another boom. That cycle has persisted as long as there has been capitalism. For years, it suited us to say that the cycle had been superseded by a 'new paradigm', but that was so much hooey. It is now okay to mention the cycle again.

But it's best not to talk about the less positive bits of the cycle. You may think it odd that the use of certain words – recession, slump, depression etc – can cause such alarm that we dare not say them aloud. It is as though they possess a malign magic power that is unleashed as the words leave the tongue. And, of course, this entire culture is dependent on another of those magic words, 'confidence'. Investors must have it, and manufacturers, and management, and – above all – consumers. Consumers must be convinced that things are basically fine, that a downturn will be quickly followed by an upturn. Otherwise, they will hoard their money; they won't spend; things will remain unsold, prices will fall, profits will fall. This will destroy any confidence that investors and manufacturers and management have, driving the economy down further.

Remember, the 11th and 12th Commandments:

In the midst of a boom: *No matter how good things get, things are about to get better!*

And in the midst of a downturn: *No matter how bad things get, things are about to get better!*

Repeat this as often as possible. Never let a chance go by to point this out to investors and manufacturers, managements and consumers.

Is it true?

Of course not. But if we all don't believe it will happen, it probably won't. Because so much depends on *confidence*.

People who buy things must be convinced that the economy will continue to support their aspirations. Otherwise they won't spend, and they won't borrow. People who manufacture, and people who sell, must believe that their profits will grow or they'll cut back borrowing and investment.

Without confidence, the thriving economy will falter; without confidence, the stagnant economy cannot grow.

The economy may be collapsing around you but, remember: 'We must not talk ourselves into a recession.' To admit that the economy is in trouble is to plunge the economy into trouble. *Belief* is what matters. If we all *believe*, we will borrow, spend, buy, make, sell, and with the help of Jesus and his Daddy everything will work out okay.

This sounds terribly like superstition, and of course it is. And there's nothing wrong with a bit of healthy superstition. Without it, we'd be all bogged down in the tedious gutter of dreary reality. In times of trouble, we must encourage ourselves to look out of the gutter and up to the sky; to see it and to reach for it.

When the downturn is unmistakable, we say that a natural and temporary dip in the economy was aggravated by unusual circumstances. While this has prolonged the dip, the economy is merely changing gears, in a transitional period on the way to a renewal of the boom. And, while the word downturn is permissible, the R(ecession) word is still a no-no. The phrase to use is, 'our current difficulties'.

It is important that when you mention a dip or a blip or a change of gears, a downturn or a glitch or a hiccup or a temporary setback, you point out that 'the fundamentals of the economy are sound'. No matter how bad things get, this phrase will give you breathing space, as it means whatever you want it to mean and so cannot be refuted.

At some stage, if you are to retain credibility, you have to stop talking about how we are showing the whole world how it's done. You again begin referring to 'our small open economy'.

Do you ever announce that the economy is entering a recession?

No, never.

What about when growth is negative, jobs are being shed like dandruff in a 1950s ballroom and everyone knows that the economy is crocked?

That is when you take a deep breath and announce that you foresee an upturn that signals an end to the current downturn.

Do you ever admit the existence of a recession?

Yes, when it's over. You can then casually refer to how our sublime ability to work our way out of the recent recession demonstrates our ability to show the world how it's done.

Those who believed your confidence-boosting assertions that there was no recession coming will assume they missed your analysis of why an unexpected recession arrived; they will be comforted to hear your authoritative announcement that things are fine again.

If asked when you think the upturn will begin, the honest answer is that you haven't got a clue; and that, of course, is something you must never say. When leaders show uncertainty there is despondency in the ranks. The correct answer is: 'About twelve to eighteen months at the outside, a good deal less if the US economy takes off'. If you say the upturn will be much sooner you won't be credible; say it will take longer and you'll damage confidence. And, in any comment you make, you must add: 'if the current indications don't change drastically'. If there's an upturn, you can point to your upbeat prediction; if there's not, keep your mouth shut. If some negativity merchant points to the inaccuracy of your prediction, you merely point out that conditions changed drastically.

You may wish to use the 'shape', or LUV, metaphor. In this, you use a letter shape to illustrate your theory about the downturn. In the L shape, the economy drops like a stone, then dawdles along at that low level, into the foreseeable future. This is nightmare territory and it's best avoided. You may suggest that a U shape is possible, with the economy dipping to a low point, staying there a while, then rising again, making a U shape. Best of all, you may suggest that while the economy undoubtedly has dipped, you expect it to hit a low point and immediately shoot back up, making a V shape. While V is the most optimistic shape, some prefer to use U, as sudden moves make entrepreneurs nervous. But anything is preferable to the L shape, which depresses the hell out of everyone.

Anything, that is, except the A shape. The A shape sees us rising to a peak and plummeting to unheard of depths, and if the A shape is appropriate we'll all be taking in each other's washing until the next millennium dawns, so – if it's okay with you – we just won't mention the A shape again.

Some believe that the shape metaphor lends authority to one's pronouncements on the economy. We don't recommend it; it is such transparent nonsense that it leaves no doubt that you're making it up as you go along.

Don't Mention Our Colonies

One of the proud and true boasts of the old Ireland was that we had a special relationship with what used to be called the Third World. After all, we had been a colony for 800 years. We had been buggered about by the British, until we bloodied their noses and they got in a huff and disowned the island (well, $^{26}/_{32}$ of it). Unlike the Brits and the French and the Dutch and everybody else, we didn't have dirty hands in dealing with Africa and Asia. We never had colonies. It's true that the Irish joined up with foreign armies, mostly the Brits, and played the imperial game, but as a nation we didn't have colonies.

De Valera and his mates were proud of that; they believed they had a special empathy with the new governments of places such as India, freed from the yoke of the crown. When we sent people abroad they carried not guns but crucifixes and rosary beads. And not all of them ended up destroying local communities in the name of the Lord. Many stood shoulder to shoulder with the poor, against the men with the whips in their hands, the guns on their shoulders and the politicians in their pockets.

Somehow, along the way, we have acquired economic colonies.

Our shops – whether they are Pound Shops on the Northside of Dublin or over-priced image shops on Grafton Street – are loaded with goods made cheaply in our colonies. We walk around in Nike gear, from the tip of our baseball hats to the toe of our Air Max trainers, made by bullied, pregnant women in Asian sweatshops, for pennies. Poor countries are plundered of their raw materials and exploited for their cheap labour. Once, we were England's source of cheap food. Now we literally grow fatter on the chocolate made with cocoa produced by child slaves in Africa (obesity in the Irish male population went from 8 per cent in 1990 to 20 per cent in 2000; in the same period, the average weight of Irish citizens went up by a stone).

Of course, our colonies are not Irish colonies. It used to be that one country formally owned a colony in another part of the world. These days, colonies – providing cheap labour and materials – are controlled by massive corporations, based in the West and spanning various national economies, including ours. Political arrangements are refereed through the United Nations, the World Bank, the IMF, the OECD, the G8 Group and the rest of the multinational managerial set-up.

Unlike the old days, the controllers of the colonies seldom have to send armies overseas to put down rebellion. Instead, the political referees employ local strongmen to manage their estates.

This New Ireland, as an economy, is an element of the Euro region, with strong links into key multinational sectors based in the USA. This combination brought us the 1990s wave of prosperity. It also brought us a minor share in the neo-colonies of Africa and Asia. And we didn't have to send a single soldier out to conquer any distant shower of nationalistic upstarts.

However, it is best, for the sake of our notions about our shiny new Ireland, not to make too much of this.

Don't Mention . . .

Don't mention Eircom. There are a lot of things we shouldn't mention about Eircom. It's best not to recall the time when it was called Telecom Éireann and its chairman, Michael Smurfit, decided they should have a new headquarters and . . . well, the past is a different country.

There was a time when Eircom was on everyone's lips. It was like a new word that had been coined specially for the New Ireland. It cost millions just to change the name of the company from Telecom Éireann to Eircom. The company had to have the new name, to celebrate its arrival in the marketplace. Eircom's six little letters spoke of Éire, this dynamic New Ireland; it spoke of the com in dotcom; it spoke of the com in communications revolution. Most of all, it spoke of easy money. No, it didn't speak of easy money: when, in 1999, Eircom was privatised, it *screamed* easy money.

The government, with the breathless support of the media, the banks and the business sector, saw the privatisation of Eircom as an opportunity to convert hundreds of thousands of citizens into stock market gamblers. Eircom shares would be flogged off at the highest price the market would bear. Those buying shares and holding onto them would get bonus shares after a year. The hype ensured that desire for shares exceeded the total available: this made an immediate price jump inevitable. The very name Eircom would come to symbolise the dynamism of the New Ireland, freed from the fuddy-duddy caution of the politically correct.

The government's consultants and advisers walked off with tens of millions of pounds, for organising this (see *Hiring the Professional Cute Hoor*). Being smart chaps, they got their money up front.

The Eircom project would create a share-owning culture, an enterprise culture. Creativity, innovation, dynamism – these were just some of the words that our newly born entrepreneurial culture reminded itself it ought to find out how to spell.

People worked hard, did overtime, had second jobs, saved, invented things, created things and sold them –

and paid over 40 per cent income tax. The entrepreneurs, in their new share-owning culture, merely had to gamble their money, and their profits would be taxed at just 20 per cent, the level to which capital gains tax had been lowered by the wealth-friendly government.

The mugs were drawn into the Eircom mess by a relentless campaign. You had to be poor or a fool not to get in on the scheme, we were told. Buy the shares, the price will immediately rise by 10 per cent; cash in if you like, and make a killing. It's like getting Saturday's winning Lotto numbers of Friday night. Or hold on until a foreign company comes in and buys Eircom and you'll make an even bigger killing.

There were two angles to the campaign. One played on greed and the desire for easy money. As long as you already had a few thousand pounds to spare, all you had to do to make a bundle was buy as many Eircom shares as you could afford. To help you, the banks reduced even further its plummeting criteria for giving credit. Some banks began contacting customers and offering loans without being asked.

The other angle was fear. Hesitate and you'd miss your chance; you would be a fool, an eejit, a loser. People would laugh at you for being so thick as to pass up a chance for easy money. Do you wanna be laughed at by the smart people, the cool people?

And a few did indeed make money, buying shares and getting out quick. But most people stayed in, as the media and the experts advised, and watched the value of their shares dive by a third, as Eircom went into a tailspin. They whined that this wasn't fair, this wasn't the way it was supposed to be. Frankly, it was embarrassing. The enterprise culture showed all the dynamism of a drunken punter walking home in the rain after the last race at Punchestown, tearing up his betting tickets, muttering to himself and letting slip the occasional sob.

On leaving the board, having seen shareholders lose a third of their investments, Eircom's non-executive directors celebrated their own success as they received 'special payments' of the order of £100,000, £75,000 and £50,000, while the chief executive (on an annual salary of several hundred thousand pounds) got a special thank you of £380,000.

Even among the losers there were winners. Professional gamblers amongst the Eircom losers could, of course, get a tax break by writing off their losses against profits from other shares. It was the mugs who were taken to the cleaners.

The mobile phone end of the business was sold off to Vodaphone, at a knock-down rate; and the biggest of the big boys, Sir Anthony O'Reilly and the Blessed Denis O'Brien, fronting for global capital, stepped in and fought it out to see who would get to hoover up the landline end of the business. In no time, a national communications system that had been built up by the state (including a modernising of the system at a cost of £1.5 billion) was transferred to private hands, outside the country.

To mention this, however, is to invite suspicion that you favour allowing the notoriously inefficient nanny state to play a role in commercial matters that should not concern it. And that would be to raise doubts about whether you are 'sound', whether you live in 'the real world'; it would raise suspicions that you might be a begrudger. Hush.

The Big Eight Unmentionables

1. Prolonged global growth
2. Billions in money transfers from EU
3. Access to huge EU market
4. American capital's need for export platforms within EU
5. Cheap labour
6. Low corporate tax
7. Pool of educated unemployed
8. Borrow, borrow, borrow, spend, spend, spend.

Mix. Shake vigorously. Stand back. *Boom!*

How to Handle a Downturn

You have already learned (see *Don't Mention the Recession*) what to say in a downturn; but rhetoric is not enough; you have to be seen to actually do something. Which is: when times are tough, you will screw the vulnerable.

That isn't advice: it's a morally neutral statement of how the world works. In keeping with our non-judgemental approach to politics, we offer here an outline of the easiest way to relieve the pressure that falls on all politicians in times of economic downturn. Downturns and booms go together like county councillors and brown envelopes. One inevitably follows another. In times of downturn, your responsibilities include knowing how to ease the burden onto the vulnerable in the most effective and humane way possible.

Why afflict the vulnerable at all? Well, to be brutally frank – which is something you, as a politician, must never be – simply because they *are* vulnerable. If you have to have a brawl with someone, it's best not to pick the biggest, burliest bruiser in the playground.

The wealthy, the comfortable classes, the people who matter, might be best suited to a little belt-tightening. You might imagine that they can most easily absorb some punishment without too much pain. However, they are also the best organised, the most powerful. They run the political parties and the media and the upper reaches of the civil service and the professions. The most powerful of them fund the political parties.

On the other hand, who are the most vulnerable? The old, the young, the sick and the handicapped.

Who are you going to pick on? Get real.

As the downturn arrives, bankers, higher civil servants, along with cute hoors by the gross, will whisper in your ear that it's time to afflict the vulnerable. It will be explained that tightening the belts of the comfortable classes just isn't on. It would cause a flight of capital, a wave of disinvestment. This would damage the economy and undermine your chances of re-election. The academics and economists, many of them the older brothers of the entrepreneurial classes, will provide the necessary independent expertise and statistical support to back this up.

Now, you will be advised that before getting stuck into the defenceless, there is quite a lot of juice to be squeezed out of what today's middle-class youngsters refer to as the *skangers*. These are working class, lower middle class, PAYE types, those who do the heavy lifting. The skangers have long experience of being squeezed, and will be half-expecting it. As long as they don't get uppity through their unions, they have little clout.

Stroke the trade union leaders with great care. Many of them, after all, are professional administrators whose career paths led them to the unions, and who might as easily have ended up as personnel officers or lower level management. In fact, many of them jump to the other side of the table in the later stages of their careers. They'll see your point of view and impress on their members the need for responsible behaviour. Again, statistical support for this, or any other line you wish to push, is readily available from the cute hoor academics and economists.

You will find it useful to impress upon the trade union types that irresponsible demands will not alone damage the nation's economic prospects, they will hurt the most vulnerable in our society.

However, squeezing the skangers can go only so far. While a certain amount of restraint can be forced on trade unionists at all levels, the more militant will kick up, and this may eventually bring trouble. So, when that route has been used to its greatest advisable extent, it is unfortunately necessary to cut yourself a little slack by trimming the budgets for the weakest: the old, the young, the sick and the handicapped.

Cutting state spending inevitably means thumping health, social services and education, as these are the high-spending departments. The comfortable classes have created their own private health system. Therefore, the scope for belt-tightening in the public health system is limitless. There is no operation that can't be put off, no ward that can't be closed, no scheduled hiring of nurses that can't be postponed. There will be complaints about lengthy queues, but this is leftwing pinko nonsense. If the skangers spend endless months queuing for treatment, what's the big deal? It's not like they're going anywhere in a hurry, is it? After all, it's not like they have better things to do with their time. (For some detail on how to make health cuts, see *How to be a Minister*.)

You must be tough but logical. Tightening belts at university level, for instance, will hurt the comfortable classes, who will express their displeasure in ways that may affect your re-election. There's nothing wrong with an extra few kids being squeezed into a classroom, at primary level, if the state has to save money. If the downturn is lengthy, many of the skangers' kids will be emigrating;

more of them will go on the dole; so, logically speaking, money spent on their education is a bit of a waste.

Brute strength alone is not enough, however. You must be humane in your brutality. You must continue to demonstrate your social concern (see *How to be Socially Concerned*). Every move must be prefaced by some remark about protecting the most vulnerable. The pose to strike is something like this:

> We regret that we all have to tighten our belts at this time; and we are aware that this will cause some suffering in the short term. However, we are doing our best to protect the most vulnerable from the effects of this downturn, which – in this small open economy – has been forced on us by events outside our control. To this end . . .

And here you announce details of some minor redistribution of resources to help the old, the young, the sick and the handicapped. This won't cost a lot – it will be a fraction of the savings achieved by the cuts. And, if you've done your job right, you'll have siphoned away more than enough during the boom period to pay for it. With this providing some cover, you can then quietly go ahead with the cuts.

Why bother diluting your cuts with a splash of humanity? To handle this without some gestures of social concern would be to build up resentment among the skangers, which might backfire later. More important, without such measures to point to, your friends among the trade union leaders would find it difficult to convince their members that restraint is necessary, for the protection of the most vulnerable.

Before you have the burden of dealing with a downturn, of course, you must reach a position of national responsibility, and that requires some instruction in the delicate art of backstabbing.

3

Climbing the Ladder

'Ambition drove many men to become false;
to have one thought locked in the breast,
another ready on the tongue.'
– *Gaius Sallustius Crispus, c.41* B.C.

Getting onto the Front Bench

You are now equipped with the information necessary to get a start in the politics business. You know the route into and up through the parties; you know the issues you must master and the ones you must ignore. You know how to explain that scandal is no longer a part of our ethical democracy. You understand the importance of the economy and you know how to explain a boom and deny a recession. You are, in short, ready to take your place among the winners.

Rank and file TDs are damn all use to anyone. It's a comfortable living, but a demeaning one, having no function other than to be re-elected over and over, always concerned only for your electoral prospects, having only the slightest acquaintance with politics. Settle for that if you feel you must. The money is good and you can pass the seat on to your descendants. However, to have any real influence, and to personally graduate to a status and financial position worthy of your talents, you need to become a minister.

First, make yourself useful to the party stars; write their speeches, praise them, ask their advice. Kiss their asses.

That won't be enough. The last thing the leaders of a political party want to see is a young, dynamic, talented, energetic new TD. Talented, energetic people are trouble. They will want to push their way to the top, which inevitably leads to someone in the old order having to make room. The leadership prefers TDs who vote in the

Dáil as they are directed, and spend all the rest of the time minding their seats.

To be taken seriously, you must build a power base. You must accumulate clout.

Make common cause with younger politicians in your own party; feel them out for discontent with the old order. With some of the young turks, you can form a long-term alliance, preparing for the day when you can rise together through the ranks, stalking the old timers and eventually chopping them off at the knees.

Others of your own generation are glorified gobdaws, whining about their betters. Encourage their discontent; push them to badmouth the party stars; suggest like-minded gobdaws with whom they can plot. Then, betray them to the upper echelons, thereby demonstrating your loyalty, your cunning, your usefulness and your readiness and ability to be ruthless.

Cultivate the rich and powerful of the business world. They, after all, have riches and power, and what else is this whole game about?

They can subsidise your career; they can, at your suggestion, bung money to other politicians. In doing so – and making it clear that it is being done at your suggestion – they boost your standing with the party's movers and shakers. The rich and powerful have influence on where, for instance, investments are sited; this can be used to your electoral advantage. Treat these people with respect, or they will treat you with contempt.

Don't buy into the fashionable notion that religion is

dead in Ireland. The Catholic Church may not be the force it was, but religion is still a power in the political marketplace. Treat it respectfully. These days, religion often turns up disguised as psychobabble about the 'Irish soul'; more often, it's the good old devotion to a favourite saint, just as in the old days. Whatever its form, your electoral prospects are enhanced if you can appear to have a spiritual side. People respect this, even though recent experience shows that many of the greatest crooks to shuffle in shoe leather have been daily Mass-goers.

In the last months before an election, make yourself visible at appropriate Masses and services. Ash Wednesday can be an occasion for a very obvious display of your piety. Those who are religious will find this attractive; those who are not will respect your open adherence to your creed. (If you're too busy and/or hung over to make it to the church on Ash Wednesday morning, remember that no one will be forensically examining the origin of the ashes on your brow.)

During election campaigns you'll need to keep track of the times of all the Masses in your constituency. Church attendances are down, but you'll find several hundred voters clustered in one handy-to-canvass assembly; be sure to set aside Sunday mornings for greeting people as they leave church.

Take up some feel-good issues and make them your own: the kind of things that no one can possibly take issue with, that don't cost a penny to rabbit on about, and that add a veneer of concern to your image. Road safety is one;

sport is another. You might decide to be strongly opposed to underage drinking. (Be careful not to alienate voting-age drunkards. The line is: 'Now, no one enjoys a few pints more than I do myself, but . . .') Showing concern for the environment can be useful, but don't get too identified with it. On occasion, when jobs are at stake because of environmental projects, you might walk into what politicians call a lose-lose situation.

No politician has ever suffered by demanding a better health service. Whenever a health issue arises, get angry about it. Particularly if you happen to be in office. *How was this allowed to happen?* you must ask, with a convincing display of rage. The implication must be that some bumbling bureaucrat in the bowels of the civil service has been heartless while your back was turned. This impression is all the more important if the problem has your fingerprints all over it.

It's all about being seen to be concerned. If you win people's trust, you have clout.

Attend every GAA, FAI and IRFU game to which you can wangle a ticket.

Seek out the committed voters, those locked into supporting the party through habit or self-interest. Stroke them.

Seek out the gobdaws, the slack-jawed ones who are easily impressed by your status. Bores they may be, but give them attention and in return for a friendly word, a handshake or a promise, they will be bound to you for life.

Seek out the floating voters; find out which are the controversial matters in the constituency, and what way the wind is blowing; blow accordingly.

Identify those committed to other parties; identify those who display a degree of independence. Identify those of your own party supporters who are in the pockets of your party's other candidates in the constituency. Then, ignore the lot of them. They won't vote for you, so they're not worth a minute of your time or an ounce of your concern.

Cultivate the party bosses. Make yourself useful. Be prepared to prove yourself by doing their dirty work. Not for too long, or you'll get a reputation as a hatchet man. Just long enough to ingratiate yourself. Prove your usefulness and ruthlessness, then show your restlessness. At that stage, the party bosses will recognise that it makes more sense to have you inside the leadership tent pissing out, rather than outside the tent pissing in – and you can expect promotion to the front bench.

How to Grab Some Glitter

Celebrity endorsements are great for enhancing image and clout. People buy clothes and soap powder when celebrities endorse them, and you'll find there is a similar effect in politics. By and large, you can't hire celebrities to back a political campaign; it needs a personal touch to get them on board.

Catch him in the right mood and Bono – an amicable chap, who likes to be helpful and is easily conned by the kind of plausible sincerity you will have cultivated by now – can be wheeled in to make a ringing political statement, such as, 'Hey, man, you know, like, cool, baby'. What Bono says isn't important; if you can get into a photo alongside him, and he's not clearly grinding his teeth, it will increase your credibility.

Boy and girl bands are also useful. On their way up, they'll stand beside anyone and grin relentlessly as long as they get their picture in the paper. Their teenybopper fans might even volunteer to distribute your leaflets, in the impossible hope of meeting their idols. The fans' parents might well vote for you on the basis that you can't be as stuffy as other politicians if these hip young folk think highly of you. There is, of course, the danger that if anyone asks them a question the guys will make it quite obvious that they haven't a clue who you are.

Sports stars can add to your glitter factor. They can be photographed with you, appear on a platform alongside you or turn up at a meeting, lending their status to your campaign.

It's always best to have the permission of these people before using them. However, it's not a strict requirement. When Jack Charlton was at the height of his popularity, a politician managed to get his photo taken with the Ireland manager at some function or other. At the general election that followed, the politician's campaign leaflets carried the picture, along with an enthusiastic call from

Charlton for a Number One for his good friend the politician. A bemused Charlton protested; the politician said there was a misunderstanding, and promised that he would withdraw the leaflet. He kept distributing it and was handily elected. Bear this in mind if you ever feel your public standing needs a shot in the arm. Turn up at sports functions and congratulate the winners. Should Bono, Joe Duffy or Mick McCarthy turn up at any function within striking distance, go for it: pump his hand enthusiastically, smile big and turn your best profile to the camera.

How to Put On the Poor Mouth

Putting on the poor mouth is an ancient Irish art. It is not enough that you achieve an objective, you must hold onto it; you must advance beyond it to make further gains. The art of putting on the poor mouth involves misdirection, disguising your ambition. You do this by casting yourself as a hard-done-by poor *crathur* who is still struggling to reach first base.

In short, you consolidate your position and advance from it by *pretending that you are still yearning to reach that position*.

For example:

The business lobby, their professional cute hoors and media groupies, maintain a persistent drumbeat demand for tax cuts. This is part of an ideology that insists there is no such thing as a good tax. The government must be got 'off the back' of business. You and your Dáil colleagues will, of course, find it necessary to back them up on this, given that the business sector pays for your election campaigns.

As it happens, the tax rate in the UK, as a percentage of GDP, is 40.9. In the Netherlands 45.4. In Germany 46.1; France and Austria 49.6.

In Ireland it's 40.2.

Nevertheless, the drumbeat doesn't waver. Similarly, the business sector persistently complains about how it is ground down with business taxes. As it happens, business taxes are light. The point of the clamour is not to push business taxes down further – though that would be nice – but to use this drumbeat to identify a sector as a special case that must be treated with kid gloves.

For the record, the percentage rates of effective corporation tax after incentives: in the UK 29, in the Netherlands 31.8, in Germany 38.5, in Austria 17.7 and France 32.8. And Ireland, 13.9.

Another example: a genuine quote from a real, live entrepreneur, explaining and applauding his own rise to riches, in a business magazine: 'Ireland in the 1980s was a communist state', with the state antagonistic to business. In fact, Ireland in the 1980s, through hard-working civil servants, provided would-be business hotshots with all sorts of tax breaks, incentives, grants and support networks. However, by putting on the poor mouth, creating imaginary obstacles he had to overcome, this guy enhances his reputation as an achiever. He also gives the impression that the flagging economy of the 1980s was a result of too many rules and regulations. The message is: *People like me should never be subject to the petty rules and regulations of an enterprise-stifling state*.

You too can use this technique. Within a constituency, for instance, you can claim to be the underdog. You may know that you are safe enough, but you can never be too careful. You can let it be known, falsely, that private polls show your seat is in trouble. This will win you a sympathy vote; it may also cause party hacks and cute hoors to rally around you, rather than another party candidate. When you retain the seat, the party hacks and cute hoors will believe they won the election for you. Thank them, sincerely. Demonstrate humility and gratitude. You may need them at the next election.

How to Launch an Election Manifesto

The function of an election manifesto is to get you elected. Therefore, it should contain nothing negative and nothing that annoys any significant percentage of the voters. It must contain nothing that commits you to a policy you can't squirm out of. There's nothing wrong with making promises, but you have to be careful to hedge them around with subtle escape clauses (*'as soon as circumstances permit'*, *'at the first opportunity'*, *'to the greatest possible extent*' etc). In short: never make a promise you can't break.

Your professional cute hoors (see *Hiring the Professional Cute Hoor*) will draw this up for you; they will cobble together the various policy documents they have written since the last election and select a list of priorities. They will isolate a selection of goodies that can be safely promised; they will wrap various promises in the kind of language that ensures you can ditch them later on, if necessary. They will work out what the various measures cost, and the income that other measures will generate, and they'll make sure it all balances. They will make up figures where necessary. It isn't important that the figures make sense, only that they don't present your enemies with an opening to stick it to you.

The result should be a richly detailed election programme that will impress the punters as you launch it in the priciest hotel conference room you can afford to hire. The detail doesn't matter; what matters is the image.

It helps to read the manifesto before it's launched. During the 1997 general election campaign, Dick Spring was asked if his Labour manifesto contained a commitment to reform the libel laws. Having taken some hard knocks from the media, Spring was in no mood for concessions. 'No', he said, bluntly. A few minutes later, a flunky passed him a note telling him that the manifesto did in fact contain a promise to reform the libel laws. Some professional cute hoor had reckoned that the commitment might generate some media support for the party during the election, so the reform had been promised. The effect was somewhat undermined by Spring's public ignorance of what was in the manifesto he was launching.

An example of how to do it was seen in the same campaign, where Fianna Fáil promised a law and order policy of zero tolerance. There had been much enthusiastic, if inaccurate, media coverage of the success of the zero tolerance policy launched by police and civic authorities in New York in the early 1990s. So, we'd have our own zero tolerance policy, said Fianna Fáil. No crime would be tolerated – none, full stop.

Asked, at the launch of the manifesto, how long it would take to implement the Comstat programme, a central element in the New York policy, the party spokesperson, John O'Donoghue, responded with a blank expression. He hadn't a clue what Comstat was, much less any intention of implementing it. It was just that zero tolerance made a zippy slogan.

Critics hadn't a chance. Anyone who queried the zero tolerance policy, including the Garda Commissioner, was asked bluntly: *What level of crime do you think we should tolerate?*

The voters bought it. And over the next five years, the level of crime fell. This was due mostly to demographics, and a costly increase in the numbers jailed. And the biggest increases were in the convictions for prostitution and vagrancy. Meanwhile, in an increasingly drink-sodden, arrogant and aggressive society, the levels of murder, rape and personal violence shot up.

Leftwing pinkoes might count the zero tolerance policy a failure. As a policing policy it was pointless. As an election tool, however, it was superb.

The trick in writing your election manifesto, once you've bulked it out with policies that no one will read, is to find two or three soundbites that catch the imagination of the punters. Doesn't matter what they mean and whether they will ever be translated into practice, the test is: will they get you elected?

What if you make a direct, unqualified promise in your election manifesto and for one reason or another you have to break it? Example: Bertie Ahern's promise in his 1997 manifesto that he would not allow any international military commitments without a referendum. The powers that be in the EU and in the US wanted Ireland inside the NATO subsidiary, Partnership for Peace. These are powers that do not take no for an answer. What's a conscientious taoiseach to do? Bertie simply broke his promise and signed up. Lesson: if there is sufficient time before the next election to allow memories to fade, there is no promise you can't break.

How to Perform Well in Opinion Polls

Much of the money gathered by political parties is spent on polling. These are not the opinion polls beloved of political junkies, but private polls designed to explore the parties' weaknesses and strengths and adjust their policies and campaigns. When you announce your firm commitment to some proposal, reform or development it will not be because you are suddenly converted; nor will it be an abrupt decision to make a principled stand on something or other (principled stands on anything are to be avoided; only amateurs can afford such self-indulgence). It will be because a private poll has convinced you that saying one thing rather than another is more likely to increase your support.

By privately researching public opinion, in the smallest detail, at national level and within crucial constituencies, you can adopt precisely the policies that you know will win public approval. If such policies are inconvenient, you can always ditch them once you're elected.

The media commission opinion polls and publish the results, and all you can do is live with the results. By commissioning your own poll, you can decide to release the results that help your image and bury the results that are damaging.

You may commission a private poll with the aim of creating a result that suits your purposes. Since you pay for the poll you get to decide what questions are asked, which can influence the answers you get. You'll find that some of the snootier research outfits will refuse to accept such a commission, on alleged principled grounds, but look hard enough and you'll find some obliging cute hoors.

Get a rhythm going, build a series of questions that invite a positive answer, then throw in the one that matters.

Let's say you want to build a massively expensive sports stadium on the site of the GPO and you're somewhat worried that public support might be lacking. An impossible project, you might think, and you might be right, but it is possible to get an appearance of support for just about anything. You might commission a poll with the following questions:

1. Do you believe that young Irish athletes deserve all the support they can get?
2. Do you believe that Irish citizens are entitled to sports facilities equal to those available in other countries?
3. Do you want the nation to have sporting facilities that reflect the greatness of its top athletes?
4. Given that current sporting facilities are hopelessly inadequate to the task, should a small percentage of the nation's resources be allocated to appropriate improvements?
5. Do you believe that all of us, whatever our background, should have equal access to sports facilities?

You have now set up a *yes, yes, yes* rhythm that would do credit to Molly Bloom. You're ready to close the sale.

6. Do you think that such a facility should be central and accessible to all?
7. Do you believe that we must look to the future as well as to the past?

8. Do you agree that our sense of history should not be allowed to act as a barrier to progress?
9. Do you support the proposal for a sporting facility, on a limited but appropriate budget, accessible to all, in the centre of Dublin?

If you can't work a positive headline out of that, you're in the wrong business.

Polls are expensive. A poll with a limited number of questions, much smaller than a research poll commissioned in a marketing campaign, can cost more than ten grand. Such costs are one reason why it is necessary to cosy up to business interests that will fund your campaigns.

There is one cheap and foolproof way of using opinion polls. It was – as far as we know – used just once by a major politician.

The media polls show your party doing badly. Down three percentage points on the last poll. You call a press conference and say that the response you're getting on the doorstep – which is where it matters – is much more positive.

These things are all about creating positive images, and if they keep hitting you with slippage in the polls it will add to the air of doom and bring you down further. So, at the next press conference, when the media polls show you doing even worse, you put on a confident smile and explain that polls are complex things that must be read properly. For instance, you say, that media poll was taken last Wednesday and Thursday, before we published our policy document on something or other. Since then, you say, *your own private polls have shown a rise in support*.

You are, of course, lying. There was no private poll – why waste money on gathering bad news? You simply invent the results. You say that not alone was the alleged slippage reversed, you're up 3.4 per cent on your last private poll.

The media scum will buy this. The media need fresh material; they are always on the lookout for 'the lead', the main news point of the day. They got a headline this morning out of the media poll that showed you in trouble. They need a new one tomorrow. They can hardly run the bad news again. They will get another headline out of this news about your private poll.

Remember, you need to provide a precise figure such as 3.4 per cent; you must sound like you've got detailed research to back this up. In a private briefing – off the record – you can let some particularly servile hack know that in some regions of the electorate the improvement was as much as 5.6. Servile hacks love this kind of detail, conveyed in private, so that they alone are getting the scoop. They will reveal next morning that 'inside sources' know that the poll contains even better news than first thought.

And you can corner another servile hack and, off the record, reveal that your party is doing particularly well among women voters.

All this might marginally affect your image and your electoral fortunes; it may even stop the rot. Even if it doesn't, it will be some days before another media poll shows your slippage continuing. You can ascribe the latest bad news to some negative event or other that happened on the day that poll was taken. Since then, of course, your own private poll has . . .

Some find it surprising that the media buy this kind of thing, but they do.

How to be For or Against Anything

Throughout your career you will be bombarded with issues that you'll be expected to have an opinion on. You'll be expected to know everything about every aspect of every issue, and to take a stand on it. Frankly, there are far more important things to do with your time. Besides, if you spend your days looking into half the issues that are thrown at you you'll end up totally confused and exhausted.

Nevertheless, you are expected to take a stand; the voters hate an indecisive leader. You must be prepared to be instantly for or against anything that comes up, and in this exercise we try to prepare you.

Are you for or against – let us invent an issue, let us call it – the cessation of discontinuance? Discussion rages as to whether the cessation of discontinuance should be encouraged, or whether it is at the root of many of our problems. Political correspondents are reporting what 'sources close to the Minister' are saying. Pressure groups issue statements and organise marches; people who matter have quiet words in the ears of lobbyists, who then invite you to lunch and tell you how important it is that you come down on the right side. Columnists abuse one another for taking a stand on one side or the other of the issue. All around you, colleagues and opponents are being pushed to take a stand.

You couldn't give a tuppenny damn about cessation of discontinuance, whatever it might be, and you could take either side. With the help of your cute hoors and party hacks, and careful scrutiny of the latest private opinion surveys, you must work out how speaking for or against this proposition will affect your electoral prospects and those of your party. You must balance this against the covertly expressed wishes of the people who matter, the people who can quietly help you out or quietly place banana skins in your path. You must then consult other major party figures, as one or more of them may have a pressing reason why the party should take a particular line. Once you have done all these calculations, you will know what position to take. The gobdaw TDs who never pay attention to any issue will be told by the whips how they should think, and the party will take a line.

Here's how to speak in favour of cessation of discontinuance:

Some, I fear, may waver on this issue, unsure of which way the wind is blowing. It is all the more important, therefore, for those of us who have the courage of our convictions to state clearly and without ambiguity where we stand. Whether it be popular or unpopular, some of us choose to take a position on principle. We may be wrong – and who amongst us can claim infallibility? – but we will be strong. And what this country needs is leaders who are not afraid to speak their minds without first checking the opinion polls.

There are those who see dangers in cessation of discontinuance, and I respect their analysis, but I say that we must take a broader view. The dangers of taking a negative attitude on this issue are far greater. Having listened carefully to the views of my constituents, my parliamentary colleagues and the various experts in the field, I have come to the unavoidable conclusion that cessation of discontinuance is a step we cannot afford not to take.

Here's how to speak against cessation of discontinuance:

Some, I fear, may waver on this issue, unsure of which way the wind is blowing. It is all the more important, therefore, for those of us who have the courage of our convictions to state clearly and without ambiguity where we stand. Whether it be popular or unpopular, some of us choose to take a position on principle. We may be wrong – and who amongst us can claim infallibility? – but we will be strong. And what this country needs is leaders who are not afraid to speak their minds without first checking the opinion polls.

While I am aware of the many reasons why cessation of discontinuance can be regarded as an inevitable, and even healthy, development at certain stages of a society's growth, I have come to the conclusion that we need to take a broader view. And I believe that in this society, at this stage, jumping headlong into a policy of cessation of discontinuance holds far more dangers than it does solutions. Having listened carefully to the views of my constituents, my parliamentary colleagues and the various experts in the field, I have come to the unavoidable conclusion that cessation of discontinuance is an imposition we can ill afford.

Whichever position you take is less important than the need to put over the image of a decisive, thoughtful, caring and courageous leader.

There will come times when you find it useful to be both for *and* against something. This is easily done. When speaking to the people who are for something, you speak *for* it; and when speaking to the people who are against that thing, you speak *against* it.

Obviously, this can only be done in certain circumstances, when the audience is limited; preferably within the party, at a closed meeting, with the media excluded. At a meeting that is deemed private, feel free to arrange to have people searched on the way in, confiscating tape recorders. Tell them it's necessary, in these uncertain times, for security reasons.

How to Hold an Ard Fheis

Once you have made your way up through the party hierarchy, you will need to ensure that your hard-won authority isn't threatened by trendy notions of party democracy.

There will be times when busybody and trouble-raising types within the party rank and file organise in an effort to influence party policy. The traditional response, which we recommend, is a programme of intimidation and expulsion. Announcing a crusade to ensure the protection of party democracy, you set about the creation of 'paper branches', complete with fictional members. These will allow you to appoint a number of extra real live delegates, carefully chosen, who will add weight to the numbers supporting the party hierarchy.

If possible, don't expel the democracy cranks. It looks bad. Instead, quietly raise subscription levels, and don't tell them. When the Ard Fheis comes around, they'll apply for delegate cards and you sympathise, telling them their membership has unfortunately lapsed, due to arrears. If expulsion is unavoidable, set traps for the troublemakers by having your supporters propose motions of support for the leadership – these amount to declarations of loyalty.

A negative vote is a gesture of disloyalty, making expulsion a pushover.

The *ard fheis* is the main party mechanism for allowing the punters to exercise the bees in their bonnets. Such outings are strictly cosmetic. Experienced politicians know that democracy is best taken in small doses. The annual conference is no place for debates, with genuine motions from delegates, conflicting points of view, argument, voting and policies agreed democratically. That looks bad on TV. An *ard fheis* must be a camera-friendly rally where the rank and file skulls are allowed cheer the party stars and let their hair down at a number of late-night parties. Anyone who says different should be immediately expelled (contact Labour; they'll show you how it's done).

The *ard fheis* is aimed at the TV cameras. The party rank and file are extras, who must cheer on cue. The seating on the platform and the order of speakers must be carefully judged for maximum exposure of those candidates who need a boost at the next election. RTÉ is deferential about these things and will act as an unpaid production company, putting its expertise at the disposal of the party and providing prime time access to viewers. (They do this out of a misbegotten sense of public duty and the hope that if they kiss the parties' backsides they won't be bullied when the party is in government – an empty hope.)

RTÉ will even provide you with a floor manager who will orchestrate the entire proceedings; a director who will choose the most flattering shots; and a commentator who will put his or her professional reputation at the service of party propaganda. This is the kind of stuff you can't buy.

Television viewers hate the *ard fheis* coverage and few watch it, but you get an hour of prime time, usually on Saturday night, so the wishes of the viewers are hardly relevant.

How to Make a Party Political Broadcast

All the rules about saying nothing of substance apply even more strictly when making the TV advert known as the party political broadcast. Unlike the *ard fheis* coverage, where you simply hog the screen for a long period of time, the party political gives you just a few minutes to hit the viewers. Impressions matter, images matter. Images of action and sincerity. These are relatively easy to fake.

The cultural undergrowth is full of professional cute hoors willing to rent themselves out to help you make the advert. They will charge little or nothing, doing it in the hope of future business. Use them for their technical knowledge, but don't let the silly buggers have a say in the final product or they'll end up trying to manipulate you.

The following is the one-size-fits-all pattern that you use, whatever your party, whatever your policies.

Positive, energetic, concerned and capable: that's the image.

Select your most photogenic candidates; exclude anyone who has appeared involuntarily before a tribunal or who has been caught with an offshore account.

Open with a series of short, sharply edited images. No shot must last longer than four seconds. At least four-fifths of the footage you use will have nothing to do with politics or politicians. An example of the kind of sequence you need:

- *A plane taking off*
- *Waves crashing on a beach*
- *A machine ploughing a field, with a rainbow in the background*
- *The party leader laughing*
- *A lifeboat being launched (symbolises the heroic party coming to the rescue of the nation)*
- *A goal being scored at an All-Ireland final*
- *The crowd rising to its feet, cheering, waving arms*
- *The party leader nodding thoughtfully, talking to a pensioner*
- *A lollipop lady helping kids across the road*
- *A candidate shaking hands on a voter's doorstep*
- *A field of wheat waving gently in the sun.*

That kind of thing. Positive, energetic, concerned and capable. Under all this there is music rising. Perhaps the theme from *2001: a Space Odyssey*. Perhaps played on a melodeon and a bodhrán.

Cut to a shot of the party leader, walking with great determination down a corridor. The party leader and the candidates should be filmed from below eye level, giving an impression of physical and metaphorical stature. Not too low and not too close, though; the last thing you want is an intimate shot up a politician's nose.

Voiceover: I come before you tonight to ask for a mandate for our caring, sincere and tough approach to safeguarding the nation's welfare.

Cut to a series of short, sharp shots, in time with the music. Positive, energetic, concerned and capable:

- *A nurse placing a bowl of flowers on a bedside table*
- *Close-up of the patient smiling*
- *A series of shots of various candidates looking concerned, thoughtful, yet optimistic; at least one of these shots should show a candidate sprinting up a staircase, to demonstrate the party's energy.*

Voiceover: This is your chance to express your trust in the future.

Cut to the party leader, sitting at a desk; there's a tricolour off to one side and there are bookshelves in the background (check to make sure there's no Jeffrey Archer novel on view).

The Party Leader: As I go from door to door I find that people – ordinary people like yourselves – are worried about the future. 'What about the future?' you ask.

And let me be the first to say that you are right. For, who amongst us knows what the future may bring?

Which is why I want you – and I'm calling on you, directly, here, this evening – to give us a mandate to protect the future.

Here, the party leader adopts what we call the Bunny Carr No.19, an expression of 'tolerance of scepticism'. This involves turning the head slightly to the right while tilting it at an angle of 12 degrees, and simultaneously raising one eyebrow and nodding sincerely. It looks simple, but it requires a lot of practice to master.

Party Leader: Now, I'm sure there are some of you who are saying, 'That's all very well, we can trust these people to be straightforward and sincere and more than competent, but what about policies?' Well, I want to put your mind at rest. We have policies. They are positive, energetic, concerned and capable policies. What's more, not only will our policies safeguard this nation as it makes its way into the future, we also have The Best Team, to ensure those policies are implemented.

A series of short, sharp shots of frontbenchers. One after the other, they are performing the following actions:

- walking quickly, energetically, urgently but confidently down a wide staircase
- playing football with a few teenage boys
- kissing a pensioner on the cheek
- eating chips out of a greasy paper wrapper, as a party worker points to a constituency map
- jumping over a garden wall
- nodding enthusiastically while in intense conversation with a uniformed garda
- sharing a laugh with a voter
- standing on the edge of a cliff, pointing out towards a sunset, surrounded by close family members.

Positive, energetic, concerned and capable.

The music is now the theme from *Mise Éire*, and the camera tracks around behind the party leader, who is sitting at a computer, rapidly typing. The camera comes right around to the front, moving in on the leader's concerned but positive, energetic, capable and – above all – sincere face.

> *Voiceover*: We need your vote, to make the future everything it can be.

End on:

- *A freeze-frame shot of a beautiful five-year-old girl smelling a flower and smiling. The party logo comes up, accompanied by the slogan:*
  Vote for the Future.

Cut. That's a wrap.

How to be a Minister

Unlike TDs, ministers have actual work to do. As well as stroking their constituents, panhandling the wealthy and preparing for the next election, they must oversee a government department.

Being a minister makes the constituency work easier; garda drivers can break the speed limit and rush you from one funeral to another, from lunch at a convent to the opening of a factory, to evening Mass, keeping the engine running while you nip in and stroke the voters. While you're off having a few jars, the state car can bring the wife and kids out to visit the missus's sister. Having a state car in which to swan around impresses the punters. They are proud of you. Most of all, they know that the county that elects a minister is a county that prospers.

Having a state car at election time is a godsend. It impresses the skulls, and your driver will be superbly trained, and very capable of avoiding pedestrians as you zoom through red lights and steam from one town to another at 90 miles per hour.

As a minister, you can bring all sorts of goodies to the constituency. You have a say in where state offices are sited, where jobs from incoming foreign companies are directed, where resources of all sorts are allocated. It is also understood that a minister can get civil servants to attend more quickly to the complaints and entreaties of constituents. Since the voters cannot be sure that another TD from the constituency would get a cabinet appointment, they will hold onto you fiercely. As a minister, you can – within just a couple of years – build up so much credit, do so many favours, bribe so many community activists and get the goods on so many potential enemies, that your seat is safe for years to come.

You would want to be caught, live on television, having carnal relations with a chicken on the halfway line at Croke Park, during an All-Ireland hurling final, before they'd get rid of you. Even then, many amongst them would argue that the chicken led you on. Much of this, apart from the state car and running a department, applies to 'independent' TDs who do a deal with a minority government. Power without responsibility.

As a minister, you will find business interests taking you more seriously. You are close to the levers of power; you are privy to government decisions that can benefit them or hurt them. You can influence those decisions; you can alert them to possible changes that will affect them.

(Please note: we are not suggesting that you *should* do any of this; being morally neutral, we merely alert you to the possibilities, based on our understanding of how these things have worked.)

You will find the wealthy taking a healthy interest in democracy. They will slip you amounts of money to be spent on your re-election; they will donate to your own campaign and to the party, directing the money through you and therefore increasing your standing within the party.

Running a department is a management function. As with management in the private sector, this involves making decisions about the work that other people have to do. It carries an amount of responsibility, but – thankfully – there are usually so many layers of flunkies between you and the outcome that dodging responsibility is easy enough.

Civil servants are the first line of defence. They take pride in their professionalism and understand that taking the rap for a minister's bad decision is part of their lot in life. Cute hoors and consultants (see *Hiring the Professional Cute Hoor*) serve similar functions.

Whether you are a fully-fledged cabinet minister or a junior minister running part of a department, the drill is the same. Your civil servants and professional cute hoors gather the information you need, make recommendations and carry your instructions down the line to the people who actually do the work (and who are always the first at whom accusing fingers are pointed). If it turns out okay, you are a hands-on minister, master of your brief, bringing innovation to a hidebound bureaucracy. If it bellyflops, you are a decision-maker, master of your brief, whose innovative instincts are sometimes snookered by the mistakes of underlings.

One thing to watch out for: civil servants and cute hoors provide the raw material to which you apply your magic touch. They can easily start making assumptions about how they are the ones who matter; they will seek to influence policy by limiting your options. This can lead to a perception that you are a mere figurehead. To combat this, it is necessary to occasionally shaft at least one of these people, rather publicly. It is necessary, from time to time, to thoroughly destroy some initiative that is too blatantly someone else's idea. It may be a good idea, in which case it is worth considering if you can steal it and present it as your own. If that is not possible, kill it stone dead. Otherwise, some might get the impression that your best ideas come from your underlings.

Now, for examples of some of the roles you may have to play:

How to be a Minister for Finance

Your function as Minister for Finance is to prudently manage the economy. Since the economy pays as much attention to you as a hormone-addled teenager does to his or her parents, you have to find ways of keeping yourself occupied.

Announcements that you are in favour of cutting taxes or keeping down public spending are always good for a headline. There may be very good reasons why taxes should stay as they are, and/or why public spending should be increased; and if you explain the necessity to maintain exchequer income in order to maintain services, you will receive wide support.

However, such policies are poison to the party's financial backers, and the academics, economists and other cute hoors on whom you depend for advice and support. Much of the media is tied to the same ideology. Bad headlines can damage your political health. Therefore, whatever the effects on services, you will always choose to cut taxes and/or public spending if at all possible; this will depend largely on how the economy behaves. The limits within which you can work are determined by a wide array of forces, both domestic and international.

Leftwing pinkoes will claim that you always favour the rich and powerful over the poor. This is not true. You generally favour the rich and powerful over the poor, for the very good reason that your political health and that of your party is sensitive to the demands of the rich and powerful. However, you are vulnerable to electoral pressure and it is necessary – in at least 20 per cent of your economic policies – to even things up a little. Go easy on the goodies for the rich in your first budget; let rip in your second and third, making dreams come through for the well-heeled set. If you are to retrieve credibility, you will need, in your fourth budget (or your fifth, if you can hold out that long), to do something about the low paid and start talking about 'looking after the most vulnerable', and about the need for 'inclusion'.

Don't worry; the rich and powerful understand why this is necessary. Only the thicker ones will call you a communist.

How to be a Minister for Education

All other ministers work within the budget allocated to them by the Minister for Finance. These budgetary limits, the decisions made by previous ministers, public expectations and the habits and prejudices of your civil servants, will leave you with a restricted and somewhat humdrum management job.

Your brief as Minister for Education is to manage a kind of gigantic people-filter. The education system consists of a number of such filters or sieves, through which young people are channelled. So many are allowed through at each stage, according to the personnel needs of the economy. So many professionals, so many engineers, so many architects; so many clerks; so many factory hands.

The background and connections of the kids will influence where they enter the system and, therefore, where they are filtered out.

This is all fine-tuned by civil servants, who liaise with the private sector and assess its impending personnel needs. Exams are used to filter out the required numbers – the marking of the exams is adjusted as necessary. The lower levels of the system deal with the greater numbers, yet at a relatively low cost. If savings are necessary, you will have plenty of slack to play with at that level, enlarging class sizes and trimming resources.

Once every few decades a major development is necessary within education. The rest of the time, it's just a matter of keeping things ticking over. Occasionally the teachers will get stroppy and you'll have to make plaintive noises about how concerned you are that the education of our fine young people will be disrupted. It always works.

Again, this is a humdrum management job. Occasionally, the nurses or ambulance drivers kick up, but you can always express concern about the old, the sick and the handicapped and appeal to the nurses' 'status' and their 'vocation'; they fall for it every time.

As this is a high-spending department, when the economy dips you can expect to have to squeeze the health service. As a politician, you will discover that the more vulnerable people are the easier they are to push around, and the less chance of a backlash; which is why the vulnerable are the first to feel the pinch. The growth of the two-tier medical service ensures that the cuts will fall largely on the weakest – the old, the young, the sick and the handicapped – which means there'll be less chance of any comeback against you.

In making health cuts, it is necessary to use certain code words. One can never, of course, simply say we must have fewer beds, or fewer nurses. Instead, attack the 'growth of administration'. You can usually produce figures that show there has been a huge rise in the number of administrators, as against little or no rise in the numbers of nurses and doctors. This shocks people, and they immediately cling to the notion that money can be saved by eliminating hordes of useless administrators who are leeching off the system. The health budget is adjusted accordingly to limit these 'administrators'.

How do you pump up the administration figures?

Simple. You re-classify social workers, ambulance drivers, lab workers etc, everyone except doctors and nurses, as 'administrators'. You then announce your intention to 'cut down on red tape'. Your budget is reduced; you leave the actual cutting to the hospital managements. They will close wards.

And so on, down through the list of ministers and mini-ministers. These are largely managerial jobs, involving occasional decisions within a fairly obvious range of options.

The big prize, of course, is to be Taoiseach. You don't have a department to run, but you get to bully everyone else. Generally speaking, ministers won't get away with anything that you, as Taoiseach, don't want them to get away with. If any minister gets uppity, you can let one of your media pets (see *How to Deal With the Media and Other Scum*) reveal that, according to a reliable source, you are considering a reshuffle. You can even leak very explicit warnings that so-and-so may soon be decorating the backbenches. That will bring them to heel.

You get to have your picture taken with foreign leaders, which can be very helpful on the credibility front (see *Ten Things to Say to the Leader of the New World Order*), but mostly you are concerned with the next election.

As Taoiseach, your party will forgive you if you embarrass it at international events. You may noisily break wind in front of the Prime Minister of Japan – no big deal. The party will forgive you if you run the economy into the ground; likewise if you invade Belgium, put the entire national budget on the 3.30 at Leopardstown or are caught snogging the Dutch ambassador in the bushes at Áras an Uachtaráin. What will not be forgiven is if you lose an election. Every commiserating pat on the back you receive will come from a treacherous hand seeking out the best place to sink the knife.

You must carefully time the general election. You must prepare an adequate war chest, by panhandling the wealthy, if necessary by doing favours you may later have to deny at a tribunal of inquiry.

With the help of party hacks and cute hoors, you will spend much of your time between elections assessing the minutiae of each region. Elections are won constituency by constituency, each one a battle on its own. The over-all campaign, fought through the media, will have an effect, but decisions made at local level are the key. When you win sufficient local fights, you accumulate the seats necessary to kick ass in the Dáil.

The party requires you to be ruthless as you assess the possibilities within each constituency. You must help the local cute hoors shaft the ambitious no-hopers, the nuts, the damp squibs and the dud relatives of the elderly TD who is on his last legs. They may believe the nomination is their birthright, but you have to be prepared to politically kneecap them.

You have to know a lot about sport; to identify the local sporting heroes and get to them before the other party leaders; sign them up for council nominations – once you've established they can read, and they can speak whole sentences without letting their dentures fall out, you begin clearing their path towards the Dáil.

Happily, not only will you have the help of the party's Amateur Cute Hoors; today, the successful politician is surrounded by capable professionals.

Hiring the Professional Cute Hoor

The country is full of cute hoors, cunning people, sly and amoral. Many of them will be your allies in your relentless march to political success. There is a breed apart, the professional cute hoor, that you will find particularly useful. These are people who have honed their cunning skills to a stage where they can hire themselves out as fixers, spinners and handlers.

A whole cute hoor industry has grown up, a new type of 'consultant' who specialises in 'interfacing' between politicians, business, the law and the voters. Use them. Their entire business is built around making you look good. They specialise in public relations, marketing, accountancy, media manipulation and personal grooming. There are also 'consultants' whose job it is to gather information and make recommendations on decisions you will have to make. These are especially useful; if the decision you make has unfortunate consequences you can always blame it on the consultants. That is their job – to take the blame. They will accept this without a quibble. Their function is to provide you with research and advice, but mostly they exist so that if necessary you can point an accusing finger at them. You should never, of course, hesitate to blame someone else when something goes wrong, but 'consultants' understand their role as fall guys. It's part of the job description.

In addition, there are cute hoors who can be 'seconded' to your team. These include economists, accountants and academics. Many of them will do occasional work for next to nothing, for the thrill of access to someone close to political power. From their lucrative but boring sinecures, they long to run the country, knowing they could do it better than anyone else, but lacking the guts to get into politics. They get all tingly at the thought of being taken seriously and having their pet theories implemented.

Tell them what you want to say and they'll put it into heavyweight language. Their status as independent specialists and intellectuals means they can be used to back your credibility. If they have qualms about your policies they will say so, tentatively, but they will swallow their qualms rather than lose their privileged access. Cross their palms with taxpayers' money. They also like to be stroked and praised. There are any number of state boards, commissions and such, to which they can be appointed. They are thrilled to be appointed to something. It makes their mammies and daddies proud of them. Without such goodies, they will sulk, believing their status is not being respected; they will mope and fret and eventually go off in a huff, later hiring themselves out to your opponents.

Lawyers are useful; they will alert you to possible legal pitfalls in legislation. They can advise you on how to threaten to use the law to nobble rivals. Their analytical minds can be of great use in figuring out the number of transfers you'll need to get a second candidate elected on the eighth count in a marginal; they can be used to write speeches and policy papers and they have enough spare, undeclared cash to be worth panhandling for a few shillings at election time. They will expect a return for this; some years later, when they have made a sufficient fortune from the law business, they will expect to be appointed to the bench. You should honour this debt; it is no harm at all to have the courts run by judges with whom the political establishment has had a mutually beneficial relationship for some years.

Business people can be useful. Many of them, from their lucrative but boring board rooms, have longed to run the country, knowing they could do it better than anyone else – and would have, had they not been too busy filling their offshore bank accounts. Appoint them to some board or other – they too just love the prestige. Such appointments show that they are not just money-grubbers, that they have finer qualities and a sense of patriotism. They can swan around, looking down their noses at their fellow entrepreneurs. (You'll also find useful helpers of this type among the ranks of journalists.)

Try not to hire too many friends and relatives for these positions; it looks bad. Unless you are the Labour Party, in which case it is expected.

How to Deal with the Media and Other Scum

Most of the time, your professional cute hoors will handle the media for you. You can't have too much positive publicity. Modesty is an over-rated virtue: nothing that is to your credit should be left unexploited.

However, if the media get no access they may turn nasty. They like to be stroked, so a modicum of contact is advisable.

Don't worry. They act tough but, in truth, they're friendly enough. It helps to give them the impression that you see them as your equal. The trick is to make them feel part of the mover-and-shaker community, a step above the *hoi polloi*, the gobdaws who just don't understand how the world works. Movers and shakers know that sometimes you have to be tough to be effective, sometimes you have to cut corners, sometimes you have to see The Bigger Picture. And all you want is mutual respect, some professional courtesy, from one realist to another. Here's the line to use: 'I'm aware that you're only doing your job, but I'm not Mephistopheles, you know.'

(That's the line for the gentleman from the *Irish Times*. For the hack from the *Independent*, this must be amended slightly: 'I'm aware that you're only doing your job, but I'm not Darth Vader, you know.')

Let them rub up against you – metaphorically speaking. Let them feel part of it all. It's easy for them to put the boot into some remote target. Bring them up-close and personal and it'll soften their cough. They can't help it. It's a common humanity thing. Flatter the scum and you'll have them eating out of your hand.

Then, give them a tit-bit, some little nugget that no one else has, maybe a bit of gossip about one of your colleagues. Something that'll get them a pat on the head from their bosses. They'll go away wagging their tails. They love to be petted. They love to be treated with respect. They love to be treated as players in the great game of politics. Cultivate such types. Give them access; use them for leaks and to gather information on your enemies, within the party and without. Play them skilfully and they can be useful: but remember you must never, ever, *ever* trust any of the bastards.

Occasionally, usually at election time, you can't avoid answering questions on major issues of the day, mostly from the media and sometimes from scummy types you meet on doorsteps, the kind of earnest know-alls who insist that you impress them with your knowledge of party policy. Don't panic, it's quite easy. The trick is to say something that sounds like it has substance, yet contains nothing that ties you down to a position; it must at the same time pander to your constituents' interests, fears and prejudices.

1. On *housing*: the soaring prices of the 1990s did, indeed, put house ownership beyond the reach of many, and although the Free Market has corrected itself somewhat the consequences of that boom remain. You are in favour of anything that broadens

the home ownership base. But we must live in the real world – prices rise because of market forces and in taking appropriate action we must be careful not to damage the equity of existing home owners. (This has a little bit for everyone; doesn't commit you to anything.)

2. On *health*: you are aware of the waiting lists and they personally distress you. You will strain every fibre to attack the task of reducing the queues. However, there are structural faults in the health service and throwing money at the problem is not the answer.

3. On *education*: young people are our greatest asset. You are in favour of education. (Perhaps tell an anecdote about a favourite teacher from your schooldays. You may not have had a favourite teacher; they might all have been abrasive scumbags. In which case, just make one up.)

4. On political *corruption*: there is no place in public life for people with low standards. You are astonished and saddened by what has been uncovered over the past few years, but you recognise that only a very small number of politicians indulged in untoward behaviour, and thanks to the excellent work of the tribunals that's all behind us now. While everyone is equal before the law, you would not wish to see a witch-hunt; anyway, all that happened so long ago and today we have Ethics. (Don't go out of your way to stress your own honesty – that should be implicit in your sad tone – and it is not necessary to deny that

you have an offshore account, except if you have one and the rumours are starting to worry your spouse.)

5. On *wage demands*: in a downturn, say – we must all tighten our belts, make ourselves more competitive, so that we can increase productivity and reach a level of prosperity from which we will all, as social partners, benefit. We mustn't make the kind of demands that will kill off our chance to escape from this downturn. During a boom, say – we must all keep our expectations at a realistic level, remaining competitive and increasing productivity so that we can protect the vibrant economy that we have built, and from which we all, as social partners, benefit. We mustn't make the kind of demands that will cause the economy to go into a downturn.

Beware of journalists who wish to conduct one-to-one interviews. They might persistently press you to explain your stance on some tricky subject.

Press conferences are much easier to handle. If an uppity hack seeks to pursue you on some issue, put on a big smile, turn to some reporter you know to be a dimwit and invite a question. If the uppity hack still seeks to pursue you, snap: 'Please don't try to hog the press conference. Give your colleagues a chance.' Shake your head ruefully and smile at the dimwit, indicating that you share his exasperation at having to put up with the antics of such a rude, arrogant hack. Look towards one of your media pets and give him or her the nod. They can be depended on to respond with such thorny questions as: 'How do you think you'll do in the marginals?' And, 'Have you any predictions about the number of seats you're likely to get?'

There is an even safer response to tricky questions. Example: the scum ask you where you stand on some issue of the day. Your answer goes something like this:

> That's a very good question. Let me be frank. When I entered politics, there were certain polit-ical choices that were simply not on the agenda. I've no wish to belittle the achievements of pre-vious generations of politicians. They worked within the parameters available to them and they did a damn fine job in the circumstances – and let me say here that I'm speaking about politicians from all parties, as well as my own. But circum-stances have changed. How can we proceed from here? Let me answer that bluntly. We live in a different world. A world of different opportunities – some of them challenging, some of them worry-ing. But some things never change. And one of those things is the commitment we must have to the citizens of this country – and especially the most vulnerable – to do our best, within the vastly changed parameters available to us, to ensure...

And you continue like this until you run out of breath. The trick is: *answer the question you haven't been asked.* And keep on going. What you are saying must have some logic of its own, it must seem to be about something of substance. It doesn't matter what it's about; the function of this answer is to put some credible words in the air, which the media scum – being a lazy shower – will mistake for an answer.

You may be afflicted by one of those persistent bastards who waits until you're finished and then says, 'That's very interesting, but the question was ...' and then hits you with it again. In which case, we refer you to Phrase 5 of *Ten Handy Phrases to Remember*.

How to Announce Bad or Good News

Saturday is best for bad news. The Sunday papers won't have time to do anything big, and – hopefully – the story will be dead by the following Sunday. If possible, use one of your media pets to break the story, ensuring a sympathetic spin. Try to find a good cause – an outing for sick children, or a birthday party for a 100-year-old constituent – at which you can be photographed that day.

Always put a positive spin on bad news. If you have to announce job losses, immediately add that you have set up a 'task force'. This will hold lots of meetings and keep the most vocal of the skangers busy so they'll drain off excess energy that might otherwise be put into giving you strife.

Good news should first be leaked via a media pet. It can then be announced in a press release. You should then hold a press conference. This is before anything actually happens. When the upbeat event finally occurs, another press release is in order, plus a photo opportunity. Six months later you can hold another photo opportunity as you 'inspect' the progress of the project. All good news should be announced at least three times, in case anyone missed it. Better still, those who heard it the first two times won't recognise that this is yet another outing for the same project and they'll assume you're never done initiating one dynamic project after another.

How to Fake Sincerity

It's best to limit your exposure to the media and other scum and say what you have to say in a formal setting. You can do this by delivering a speech to an audience of party hacks, at a constituency selection convention or an *ard fheis*. It is an audience of the faithful. You control the microphone; you can drown out any maverick who seeks to interrupt you. You have stewards strategically placed, to nobble anyone who might interrupt.

Your retinue of professional cute hoors must include specialists who will advise you on the artifice necessary in public speaking. Did you know that the average length of applause for public speakers is eight seconds? There are people who measure such things, and they can show you how to generate such applause and manipulate it. They can show you how to pace a speech, and how to construct the speech using such techniques as three-part lists, balanced contrasts and measured pauses. It is possible to create applause by the use of cadence, planted primers and buzz words. Not to mention an audience seeded with your close supporters. And, don't forget, when your audience applauds it will look impressive if you sometimes continue speaking through the clapping, perhaps even raising a hand as though to appeal for quiet. It gives the impression of sincerity, suggesting that you care more about getting your message across than accepting plaudits. Such humility will, of course, gain you far greater plaudits in the long run. For such insights, your cute hoors are worth every penny of the taxpayers' money you spend on hiring them.

The content of your speech is not of great importance; usually, it will involve shuffling around a few of the standard phrases about progress, equality and inclusiveness; about dynamism, innovation and competitiveness. It is not necessary in Irish politics to think about the problem of marshalling your arguments and convincing your audience; what matters is that you come across as sincere. Voters also like to believe that their leaders are good speakers, in the sense of good performers. Party supporters like to take pride in their party stars; they like to know that you are capable of holding your own in a slagging match with the enemy. Practising in front of a mirror is an under-rated technique.

For formal speeches, where it is essential that you perform at your best before a large audience, particularly if the speech is being televised, you are advised to use a prompter. Almost all politicians of any significance use them for key speeches. The prompter is a machine that projects your speech onto two sheets of glass, set at an angle a few feet in front of you. The words are reflected from the glass and are invisible to anyone but you. This gives the impression that you're looking out at the audience, maintaining all-important eye contact. You alternate between the two glass screens, switching back and forth from one to the other, so you're not simply staring ahead of you. The effect is that you're not reading the speech; you're making it up as you go along. In the business, these are known as 'sincerity machines'.

Your close supporters should be scattered among the audience, but a number should sit near the front. As you finish, they will stand up and stay standing, clapping furiously. Unless your rivals have seeded the audience, this should encourage the rest to get off their arses and give you a standing ovation.

How to Trickle Down

Leftwing pinko types might conclude that the New Ireland is all about mindless greed and sharp practice. Not at all. Greed, certainly; and a certain amount of sharp practice. However, there's nothing mindless about it. There is a far-sighted ideology underpinning the hustling and the backstabbing. A set of worked-out theories. A philosophy, one might say. It was thought up by highly paid intellectuals, who are paid highly to sit around all day thinking up things. You will be expected to defend it.

It goes something like this:

It's all very well being full of compassion and decency and that kind of stuff, but it doesn't work. Planning the economy leads to bureaucracy, laziness, lack of competition, stagnancy. The state's efforts to ensure equal opportunities in education, health and work may be well intentioned, but they kill initiative. Fairness and equality are fine ideas, but in the real world we have to go with what works.

And what works is people looking out for their own interests. We must remove all obstacles to business; we must deregulate everything; we must encourage competition and free up the entrepreneur to make as much profit as possible. Instead of the 'dead hand' of the state, we must grasp the 'invisible hand' of the Free Market. We must abandon outmoded trade union attitudes.

Then, in this Free Market, the entrepreneur – looking out for his own self-interest – will come up with innovative and imaginative ways to make profits; the best entrepreneurs will compete with each other, fighting to grow, to survive. This will stimulate the economy and create jobs, with the invisible hand of the Free Market ensuring that supply will meet demand, that profit will unleash creativity, that all will work out for the best.

It is, therefore, the role of the state to facilitate business. It must do so through tax breaks; tax cuts; deregulation;

laws that limit the freedom of trade unions; subsidies for education that is geared not to the wider and deeper needs of students, but to the immediate needs of business. Business must be pampered. The easier it is for the elite to make money, the more active they will become, creating more wealth. This wealth trickles down through the economy, to the middle class, the professionals, the service industries, manual labourers and what we now call the 'underclass'. A rising tide lifts all boats.

This is the trickle down theory.

There is an image sometimes used to make the trickle down theory more easily understood.

Horses and sparrows. The horses are the people who matter. The sparrows are the underclasses, the skangers, those who do the menial chores and heavy lifting.

The more oats the horse gets to eat, the more abundant is the crap it leaves on the road. And the bigger the piles of crap the sparrows get to pick through, the greater their chances of finding undigested oats to survive on.

This is known widely as the trickle down theory. To some it's known as the horseshit theory.

How to be Socially Concerned

There is a danger, as you relentlessly advance the interests of your party, its generous supporters, the nation in general, and your own well-being in particular, that you will be seen as a self-centred, pushy bundle of energy, with the social awareness of a turnip. You must show that you are socially concerned. To some, this comes naturally, as they do indeed have scruples. However, while scruples can help your image, they are such a handicap in so many areas of political life that, on the whole, one is better off without them.

In the absence of scruples, you must make other arrangements. It is not enough to throw in the odd remark about 'social justice and so on', while yawning and looking at your watch. You must sound sincere. You must learn to pepper your remarks with buzzwords that suggest you not only have a conscience about social injustice but an urge to do something about it.

You must say how important it is that we have an 'inclusive' society.

You must refer repeatedly to 'those less fortunate'.

You must proclaim your determination to do something for 'the most vulnerable in our society'.

Because you want us to 'invest in the future'.

What is the nation's 'greatest asset'?

Young people are our greatest asset.

And when should you amend that observation?

When you are speaking to older people. At which time you should adjust the remark to: 'People are our greatest asset.'

It isn't too difficult to appear socially concerned. You will find that most of your colleagues manage the trick with ease. What is important is that you give an impression of social concern without committing yourself or your party to any definite course of action.

How Not to be Too Socially Concerned

In creating your image of social concern, it is important that you not go too far. Otherwise, people will start quoting back at you what might appear to be commitments: and commitments, like principled stands, are self-indulgent treats that the serious politician must avoid. You must practise a tolerant but scornful smile and rehearse such remarks as, 'Well, perhaps I'm being politically incorrect, but . . .', as you stand up for a reasonable measure of inequality.

To this end, take heed of the following *Ten Rules of Political Incorrectness*:

1. Anyone indulging in demands for excessive commitment to fairness and decency is being 'politically correct', and may be dismissed with a sneer.
2. The poor are no longer with us; they are now 'the disadvantaged'. The disadvantaged are not 'poor'; they are merely 'less well off', suggesting that they are doing fine, if not quite as well as the average company director.
3. People who get too heated about sexism, racism or any other -ism 'have no sense of humour'.

4. People who dwell on troublesome social issues, demanding that something be done about them, should be derided for wanting to 'throw money' at problems.
5. Your opponents are 'naïve' and live in 'an ivory tower'.
6. You are 'realistic' and live in 'the real world'.
7. Anyone seeking political support for an issue that causes you problems is 'divisive'.
8 Anyone demanding action against profiteering is 'doctrinaire', and 'ideologically motivated'; you don't have an ideology, you have 'principles'.
9. Anyone campaigning on social issues may be dismissed as being part of 'the poverty industry'.
10. Those who are too insistent on such things as 'justice' and 'fairness' are motivated by 'the politics of envy'.

How to Speak Confidently and Say Nothing

When speaking to a crowd, find a friendly face in the audience and make eye contact; adopt a confident tone and try, even when dealing with some obnoxious little shit, to maintain an interested, concerned expression.

It helps to rid yourself of any bees you may have in your bonnet – in short, if you have any pet policies, ditch them. By and large, policies don't win votes, even from people who agree with them; but they lose votes, as the people who hate those policies will go out of their way to vote against you. Yammering on about your policy on this or that is a turn off. You certainly have to say things about various issues (we'll cover some of them later), but in as vague and meaningless a way as possible, without committing yourself to any specific action. You are for democracy, fairness, honesty, freedom, justice and all that sort of stuff. You're against tyranny, injustice, corruption, dishonesty etc etc etc. Try not to get any more specific than that.

Example 1: you may be asked if something should be done about such-and-such a problem.

Of course it should, you answer. *We must be prepared to put measures in place, as soon as possible. Such measures include:*

And here you reel off your policies. Bad move. Those who want something done about the problem may agree with your policies, or may not. There will be others who don't care much about the problem, who may see your policies as possibly affecting them in some way. They will, therefore, see you as a threat, and vote against you just to be on the safe side.

Example 2: you may be asked if something should be done about such-and-such a problem.

Of course it should. This is a problem that – perhaps in ways we don't yet fully recognise – concerns us all, and we must be prepared to do all we can to solve it. There you are, a nice harmless answer that will do you no damage whatever.

If anyone asks you where you stand on housing, employment, education or health – you're in favour.

You're against homelessness, unemployment, ignorance, disease and death. It isn't necessary or advisable to go into any greater detail than that. Remember, if you can't waffle on for twenty minutes on any subject without saying anything in particular, you lack a vital component in the make-up of a successful politician.

Suppose some busybody is dissatisfied with your all-purpose answer and presses you, demanding to know what measures you will propose to solve the problem. Easy: *appropriate measures*. This will satisfy most people.

The busybody keeps pushing. What exactly are those 'appropriate' measures that you will propose? Easy: *those measures will be decided after full consideration is given to all aspects of the problem, and following extensive consultation with all parties affected.* As you finish, invite another question from someone else. Should the busybody seek to push you further, adopt a pained expression and say: 'Really, you and I could continue this all evening, but I don't think we should monopolise the occasion. How about we continue this later, in private?' When the sucker approaches you later for that private chat, you are – unfortunately – late for your next appointment.

Ten Handy Phrases to Remember

1. I never said that (to be used when some piece of media scum accurately quotes something you said, but

which you now regret, and there is no audio or video tape evidence of you saying it).

2. I was quoted out of context (as above, when you suspect there is a tape).

3. I've already dealt with that matter, next question please (when the media scum attempts to play the tape).

4. This is too important a subject to use as a political football (to be used when confronted with a demand that you take a principled stand on a controversial issue).

5. I've already made my position perfectly clear (to be used when you have no intention of answering an awkward question).

6. That's a very good question (to be used when the interviewer is an easily-flattered fool, to encourage his delusion that he's asking intelligent questions).

7. This is further evidence that we have struck a chord with the voter (to be used when the opinion poll results are good).

8. The only poll I pay any attention to is the election itself (to be used when the opinion poll results are bad).

9. That's not the reaction I'm getting on the doorstep (to be used when the opinion poll results are *really* bad).

10. As soon as circumstances allow (to be used when you are trapped or forced into making a commitment to a policy – this allows you to put off action indefinitely).

Seven Precautionary Rules to Remember

1. Never say anything on the telephone that you wouldn't want to see on the front page of the *Sunday Independent*.
2. Never put anything on paper, disc, film or tape that you are not prepared to see Charlie Bird reveal on RTÉ's nine o'clock news.
3. Buy yourself a good shredder.
4. Always assume that any microphone in sight is on, and the tape is running.
5. When there is no microphone in sight, assume it's hidden.
6. The camera is your friend, provided you have control of the negatives.
7. There has never been a reporter born anywhere on this planet who hasn't had a deep, secret wish to bring a government minister to his or her knees, and that goes double for the crawlers who suck up to you.

How to Apologise

No matter how careful you are, there will come a time when you will be caught in some indiscretion and there will be demands that you apologise. Your opponents will sneer, the media scum will drool. It may stick in your craw to bend to their will, but if you don't give them something to chew on, the drumbeat will get louder, until it becomes a call for resignation. An apology is easy. Make it a non-apology.

Here's what you say:

'I'm sorry …'

And that's all they'll hear, and they'll smile smugly. You continue:

'… that some have found my actions offensive. It was not my intention to cause such offence.

When examined, there is no apology for anything you have done. You are merely saying you are sorry you are in this position. And implying that it's because some stuck-up, humourless people have found something offensive in actions that are perfectly innocent. It bears sufficient superficial resemblance to an apology to ensure that if they complain they'll look like nitpickers.

When your offence has been somewhat more serious, you may want to try this non-apology: 'I am genuinely sorry that my actions, however inadvertently, should be a source of embarrassment to me or my party.'

Again, this is no more than saying you are sorry you have been put in an embarrassing position. No apology for anything you've done. And the 'genuinely' is a nice, meaningless touch.

Try not to smirk, but this is one of those occasions when you may yawn and look at your watch as you tonelessly mutter your 'apology'.

What to Say about Europe

Europe used to be handy for politicians. If you wanted to give yourself a boost, you just demanded something or other for your constituency. Didn't matter what: a factory, a hospital, services, more TV channels, greater life expectancy, whatever. Someone would say that this would cost a lot of money, the government couldn't afford it; so, you demanded that it be funded by the European Union or 'common market'.

To some, the EU might be about tying France and Germany up in so many commercial tangles that they never again start kicking the bejayzus out of each other, as they did in the nineteenth and twentieth centuries; the 1939-45 conflict alone cost 40 million lives. To others it might be about building a continental bloc that could stand up to Russia or the USA or China. To us, it was a handy cash cow.

Part of the project of creating a large economic and political bloc involved ironing out the vast differences between developed economies and stunted little outfits like the old Ireland, so they transferred billions to us.

As long as the money flowed, we were firmly committed to 'the European Ideal', whatever it was. Anyone asking about our loyalty to the European Ideal needed only to be referred to our relentless commitment to the Eurovision Song Contest. What more proof could there be of our continental consciousness?

Come the date when the cash transfers from the EU

slowed down, and we were told that it wouldn't be long before some of our money would have to flow towards the even more stunted economies of Eastern Europe, and we began to look more closely at the European Ideal, whatever it was.

By then we were mid-boom, and feeling feisty. Sovereignty began to matter; fiscal independence, stuff like that. *By Christ, no bloody German is going to tell us how to frame a budget!* When the lousers gave us so few votes at the Eurovision Song Contest in 2001 that we failed to qualify for the following year's contest, that put the tin hat on it.

You could hardly blame us. Our entire relationship with Europe was based on receiving money. Our only other experience of the EU was when we had to jump out of the way, as visiting EU dignitaries were whisked from one engagement to the next in speeding limousines, their police escorts' sirens blaring as they zoomed past traffic lights on red.

So, slagging the EU became fashionable for a while. However, you have to be careful about this. These are powerful people, and many's the favour we'll be looking for down the line. It's best not to say anything about Europe, but some media scum might corner you so you'd best be prepared to say something.

Say: *While committing ourselves fully to the European Ideal, whatever it is, we are confident that our European friends will maintain a healthy respect for national sovereignty.*

With an eye on the *Irish Times*, which loves this sort of thing, you might say something cute about how we should *render onto Brussels that which is Brussels', and render onto Merrion Street that which is the Department of Finance's.* Above all, point out that your constituency is long over-due its proper share of factories, hospitals, services, TV channels, greater life expectancy, whatever.

What Not to Say About the North

The North used to be handy. Decades ago, you could make a belligerent speech about the need to regain the Fourth Green Field and you could rely on being carried shoulder-high. Then they started killing one another in serious numbers and the occasional bomb or bullet came across the border. That was uncomfortable, so mouthing off about the Fourth Green Field went out of fashion.

The North was still handy. You could denounce violence, wringing your hands and tut-tutting. That way, you could brush up your image of compassion, without having to confront the underlying sectarianism from which the conflict arose. This came in especially handy for some people who needed to distract attention from the fact that their own hands had been more than a little blood-spattered when it suited them.

Once the ceasefires arrived, for the general populace there wasn't much to say about the North. The usual line is that we must all work together for a lasting peace, wherein all traditions are accorded equality of esteem etc etc etc.

Those words have different meanings, depending on who uses them. In today's Ireland, the translation goes something like this:

There are Northern nationalists who still look to the Free State as a homeland that will someday, somehow, come and rescue them from the grip of perfidious Albion. And there are unionists who declare in tones of anger that they will shed the last drop of their blood before they will allow the South exert its will over 'the province'.

The delicate truth about The North, as a political issue, is that few in the South feel inclined to give a damn. While there is among some – and not just the older generations – a belief that the North is unfinished business, few see it as a priority. There is among others a genuine but vague feeling of duty towards Northern nationalists, a fear that they might again endure the kind of unionist sectarian pogroms that blasted the Catholic ghettoes in the past. And a genuine but vague feeling of duty to protect unionist traditions and reject the nationalist sectarianism that facilitated callous slaughter.

When unionists stamp their little feet and tell us they will never – *d'ye hear me, never!* – surrender their birthright to the Pope's battalions in the South, the response is more often than not a shrug. *Sure, Bosco, no problemo.* And the truth is, far from longing to invade the Shankill and wrest their birthright away, most of us wouldn't take it as a gift.

There was a time when the North meant our separated brethren. Now, it means that bloody crowd up there, screaming obscene abuse at one another at the best of times, always poised to do the unspeakable.

It wasn't just religious differences that brought about partition. There were real economic differences underlying the division. They were far more industrially developed up there; leaving the union with Britain would have been economically disastrous. Today, with the North on the economic periphery of a troubled British economy, there are real economic reasons why a united Ireland would make sense. But, regardless of economic interests, the political structures and attitudes that have evolved around unionism over the past hundred years have taken on a life of their own.

And, face it, folks, for the New Ireland, the snarling unionist and the obsessed nationalist are just so ... uncool.

It's a very obstreperous little place, the North. No end of trouble. Some amongst our entrepreneurial classes might feel some stirrings of interest when they contemplate the Fourth Green Field – after all, property has long been cheaper up there, and portfolios have quietly accumulated. Since the ceasefires, opportunities have arisen to make another kind of killing altogether. For most of us, though, the North long ago stopped being the jewel in anyone's crown.

The louder the unionists bawl about their determination to protect their birthright the more it sounds like a desperate effort to convince themselves that anyone –

whether in the South or in Britain – cares enough to want to either take over their bloody little statelet or defend it from its supposed enemies.

There is genuine regard for those – republican and loyalist – who managed to achieve the ceasefires; but puzzlement at the slowness of progress towards a sustainable non-sectarian compromise. Compared with conflicts elsewhere in the world – in Rwanda or the Middle East – it's a fairly limited problem. But there always seems to be just enough people eager to go a few more rounds.

As a politician, you will find that any definite position you take on the North, no matter what it is, will drive away twice as much support as it attracts.

So, although it is an intensely political matter, there is in the South a concern to keep the North to hell out of politics. This may be a partitionist position, but it is a consequence of decades of arrogance, violence and uncompromising hatred. You will find a widespread attitude amongst your constituents, an attitude to which you must be sensitive. It goes like this: If we can help, well and good, but don't drag us into your shrill little battle. And for Christ's sake get on with it.

Of course, one must be careful not to say anything of the sort out loud.

Therefore, let us repeat that we must all work together for a lasting peace, wherein all traditions are accorded equality of esteem etc etc etc.

Ten Things to Say to the Leader of the New World Order

1. Yes, Mr President.
2. Of course, Mr President.
3. Immediately, Mr President.
4. I hope you don't mind, Mr President, if I comment on how enchanting the First Lady looks tonight.
5. Great idea, Mr President.
6. I'll get right on that, Mr President.
7. Your courage and wisdom are an example to us all, Mr President.
8. You betcha, Mr President.
9. Would you like fries with that, Mr President?
10. Have a nice day, Mr President.

How to Be No More Racist Than is Strictly Necessary

This is an issue on which it is inadvisable to speak plainly. For instance, though you may benefit electorally from supporting measures that put the boot into immigrants, it is not recommended that you make blatantly racist statements in public. Plainspoken racism looks ugly in black and white, if you'll pardon the expression. Even racists don't want to be seen as bigots.

Instead, you must put an anti-racist statement, plain and direct, on the record. Draw attention to it in the appropriate quarters. That covers your ass. Then, you can vote for and support any amount of racist measures, and bring these to the attention of your racist constituents – they, by the way will not take offence at your anti-racist comments, should they become aware of them: they know that it is sometimes necessary, in these matters, to speak with your fingers crossed behind your back.

After decades in which we were inward looking, isolated and proud of it, Ireland at last came to look something like the rest of the world. Suddenly, there were African, East European and Asian people all over the place. New accents, new foods, new styles, new experiences, new ways of looking at things.

Obviously, that state of affairs couldn't be allowed to continue.

As a politician, you will be aware that immigration invigorates a society, culturally and economically. People desperate to escape a dangerous or stunted life bring a sense of striving to any society. Rundown areas become vital again; we get new insights into old problems; music and painting and writing are stimulated. We learn new things to do with food. As a politician, you will be aware that it was inevitable that we would receive some splashes from the massive waves of immigration surging around the globe. As a politician you will be aware that vicious upheavals in a number of regions have set millions of refugees running for cover. As a politician, you will be aware that immigration is an inevitable part of a global economy that has deep inequalities. You will understand that our boom derived from our connecting into the global economy. And that the same connection brought us the immigration, and that we can't have one without the other.

However, that doesn't mean we won't try to do precisely that. As a politician, a percentage of your voters will be uncertain of the future, scared of change or downright racist, and they too have votes. You have to cater to them.

We were for a long time virtually alone among European countries in not having a hard right political party with skinhead supporters and baphead policies. That might not have been unrelated to the fact that we had few African or Asian immigrants. Other countries had decades of a head start in developing a tradition in bigotry. There will be some who will argue that there is a history of racism against travellers, but you can forcefully argue that that isn't racism, it's just prejudice.

Whatever: the point is, when it matters, we know how to react. As a politician, you will be aware that sixty years ago, when the worst savagery in human history was rampant at the heart of Europe, we managed to avoid taking in more than a handful of Jews on the run from the Nazis. In recent decades, as smaller but equally deadly savageries erupted in various parts of the world, and as global economic fluctuations caused populations to ebb and flow, we have assumed a tough stance, lest too many immigrants with foreign beliefs dilute our Christianity.

In October 2001, we sent John O'Donoghue, our Minister for Justice, off to an international anti-racism conference in South Africa, to explain that we abhor the very idea of intolerance. On the way, John took time out to sign an agreement with the Nigerian government. We would give them £9 million. And they would help us to fast-track the expulsion of Nigerian immigrants. Some leftwing pinkoes tried to make a connection between the £9 million bung and the agreement to make it easier for us to kick out immigrants, but John explained with great sincerity that as far as he and the entire Irish establishment are concerned, racism is evil and we all abhor it. Learn from this man, one of our most successful politicians.

Even your racist constituents won't balk if, in boom periods, you support importing workers from places like the Philippines, to fill vacancies on contract. That way, we can pay them less than Irish workers get for the same work, charge them 'fees' for coming over, house them in kips and sack them if they complain or try to join a union. As they are on contract, we can tell them to bugger off out of it whenever the economy dips or we have no further use for them.

Of course, as a politician, you can't be blatant about supporting racist measures, so you have to come up with something that sounds plausible. Here's what to say:

> Yes, indeed, we have obligations to genuine refugees; but many of these people are economic migrants. Genuine refugees flee their countries

because of danger to their physical well-being.
And while we may sympathise with people who
resent having to sell their labour at slave rates,
in order to feed their children, or who fear their
15-year old daughter will end up forced into prostitution – they are not genuine refugees.

The beauty of this is that there is no identifiable racist
remark, yet it endorses policies that will allow in as few
immigrants as possible. And, if they get in, make it as easy
as possible for us to throw them out.

Here's another good line:

We must not allow the rights of genuine refugees
be diluted by the impact of economic migrants
posing as refugees.

The essential word is *genuine*. Are they *genuine* refugees?
Okay, so you say half your family were murdered: prove it.
*Okay, so you've got injuries that suggest you haven't been
as well treated as some might think desirable, but how do we
know they weren't self-inflicted?*
The trick is to raise sufficient doubt about the claim of
alleged, supposed, so-called torture, without going so far
as to openly suggest that perhaps these people did something to deserve it. The trick, in short, is to be no more
racist than is strictly necessary.
Of course, once they're back home, suffering whatever
violence or privation comes with their non-white, under-

class status, we – being mindful of our Christian duties – can perhaps organise a fund-raising concert for them.

How to Spend Other People's Money

Around 1997, after about three years of economic boom, it began to dawn on some of the people who matter that they had their hands on immense amounts of loot. From then, until the economy faltered in 2001, opportunities were taken.

Sure enough, it wasn't their money; it was money amassed by the state, harvested from the hard work and the prolonged belt-tightening of the citizens. In theory, it was the state's task to administer that money even-handedly, for the benefit of the community. There was no shortage of things – schools, health, public services, the ghettoes – that needed money spent on them. And, let it be said, the state duly did an amount of spending of that sort. However, we are but human and the temptation was too much.

Parallel with an enormous increase in private borrowing and conspicuous consumption, the political classes felt free to spend whatever public money was necessary to give life to their wishes, whims and long-held fantasies. That period is instructive. You may feel similarly inclined in similar periods of boom while you are in public office.

Wouldn't it be nice, we thought, to have a monument in O'Connell Street, in Dublin, where Nelson's Pillar stood so long ago? It would make a statement about the New Ireland. The best idea we could come up with was a long, thin, stainless steel pole, sticking straight up. This, we said, would be a 'brave and uncompromising beacon [that] reflects a confident Ireland in Europe'. Many claimed they just saw a long, thin, stainless steel pole. It cost three million pounds, and was two years behind schedule, because of an unfortunate screw-up in the planning procedures, but we insisted on making our statement.

Three million was loose change.

Farmleigh House, a 20-bedroom mansion, was put up for sale by the Guinness family. It was of no great architectural interest, having been erected in the nineteenth century as a piece of braggery by a family showing off its wealth. The government hesitated at first, then – fearful of media jibes that it lacked an aesthetic appreciation of beauty – it shelled out. And, having bought it, the government wasn't sure what to do with it, but Taoiseach Bertie Ahern reckoned it'd come in handy for something or other. The asking price was £15 million, but the government managed to get it for £23 million. We won't dwell on how they managed that neat trick. After they bought it, the cost went up by another £18 million when the house turned out to need a lick of paint. It was decided that the rejuvenated house would provide a fine bed-and-breakfast to impress visiting dignitaries.

Only a philistine would ask *why* the house was bought; we bought it *because we could*. Although the house was of little historical or architectural value, and the taste with which it was dolled up was questionable, the point was made: we have the clout. And anyone daring to question the splurge could be denounced as an unimaginative, killjoy begrudger who lacked confidence in our national greatness.

The theatre crowd had never been too happy with the acoustics in the Abbey Theatre. They too saw their chance. The only thing bothering them was: should they look for £50 million to refurbish the place where it stood, or £100 million to build a state-of-the-art building on a new site? It's known as an artistic dilemma.

The TDs needed bigger offices; no bother, here's £25 million.

Perhaps most troublesome in this period was Bertie Ahern's personal dream – an 80,000 seat national stadium, set amidst a 'sports campus'. Bertie had dreamt up this project along with some pals from the business world. Since the members of a cabinet never go to sleep or wake up without having the word *reshuffle* flutter menacingly through their minds, the proposal was rubber-stamped without question.

It was a £230 million project, or maybe £350 million. Then it was deemed to be a £750 million project. When other bits and pieces were added, some said, it would be a billion pound project. But it would be a state of the art facility – and it would have its own velodrome, whatever that was, so it was worth it.

Did we need a Bertie Bowl, asked the sceptics, complete with a velodrome, whatever that was? The government had already chipped in £25 million to support the GAA's £60 million refurbishment of Croke Park. The FAI was given £87 million to drop plans for its own stadium and agree to play at the Bertie Bowl.

When the GAA realised it had got just £25 million for re-building a stadium and the FAI was getting £87 million of taxpayers' money for not building one at all, it came back with its hand out and got another £60 million.

So, the GAA and the FAI were happy, which is when the rugby chaps came forward with *their* hands out, and big smiles on their faces . . .

The line that was peddled was a wee bit risky. The stadium wasn't about sport, it was about patriotism. Bertie sent one of his ministers out to tell the populace that the Bertie Bowl would ensure that we could 'stand proud among the nations of Europe'; it would allow us to 're-position ourselves as a people'; a national stadium would stop us being 'second class citizens'. There might be patients on trolleys in the hospital corridors, and rats in the walls of the prefabricated schoolrooms, but we'd have a bigger stadium than anything the Belgians had. Only when evidence of soaring costs coincided with the run-up to an election were the brakes put on.

There were some tricky moments. Questions, for instance, about whether the fire brigade service was up to date. Would it have to stand helpless, watching a man drown in a freezing canal in the heart of Dublin city because it didn't have the equipment necessary to reach down and pull him out? Answer quietly, yes, that's what it had to do. Were we sending our children to rural schools on ramshackle school buses, some of which were unsafe? Yes, we were. Yes, we are. Were gardaí serving the public in rural kips that were unfit for human habitation in the nineteenth century, when some of them were built? Yes, they were, and they are.

It is instructive to see how the professional cute hoors and their media groupies dealt with this. Damn it, they raged, after all those grim years, are we condemned – as long as there's a single person on a single hospital waiting list – to refrain from spending a few shillings on art, sport and a much-needed aesthetic face-lift for the nation?

Lesson: a person who matters is always ready to take the ball on the hop.

4

When the Going Gets Tough

'That's not a lie. It's a terminological inexactitude.'
– *White House Chief of Staff, Alexander Haig*

When the Going Gets Tough

How to Accept a Bribe

It is your democratic duty to accept chunks of money from wealthy business interests. Disregard the catcalls of leftwing pinkoes. Without regular injections of cash you can hardly be expected to maintain the political career that has so well served the nation. And without that career, is the way not open for the advance of totalitarianism? And who is to give that cash if not wealthy people?

As we have made clear, our advice is non-judgemental. It is your choice as to how to approach the issue of touting for donations. Who you ask, what you promise, how you spend the money – these are for you to decide. We merely outline the possibilities.

Traditionally, such chunks of money are called 'corporate donations'. However, due to the unfortunate interpretation that has been put on some of these, some politicians are a bit windy about being seen to accept bulky envelopes from business interests. For instance, in 2001, Fine Gael decided that they would no longer accept corporate donations. So, they promptly wrote to all their corporate donors and asked if they could please forward their corporate donations dressed up as personal donations from individual business people. This is precisely the kind of fresh thinking that is needed in Irish politics.

There are instances of people simply offering politicians straight, unmistakable bribes. The money is passed along, the briber states his requirements, and the bribee gives an assurance that he'll do his best to comply. Some-times the favour gets done; sometimes it's not possible. In which case the bribee will usually seek to make up for this at a later date, in connection with some other matter. Such politicians, after all, have principles: they like to give value for money. Otherwise, they might get a bad name among the bribery set.

Only the truly vulgar are so crude. The more refined amongst us seek to preserve an amount of self-respect. And that's pretty hard to do if someone stuffs a bundle of cash into your breast pocket while muttering out of the corner of his mouth, 'You'll see me right, then, okay?'

Instead, you must seek what we all agree to call 'a legit-imate political contribution'. This money comes from those who want to 'support the democratic process'. The money can be paid to a politician or to a party. Politicians traditionally make a distinction between 'political contri-butions' and 'personal contributions'. Should you ever have to argue the case, it goes like this: if you give a politician thirty grand and he spends it on a conservatory at the back of his house, that's a bribe. Give him thirty grand and he spends it on getting himself re-elected to a job that pays him ninety grand, out of which he builds a conservatory at the back of his house, that's a 'legitimate political contribution'.

It is advisable to keep records that show that 'political donations' were spent for political purposes. Whether those records reflect reality, or they are something you had an obliging accountant run up over the weekend, is no one's business but your own. Should it be discovered that 'political donations' ended up in your personal account, simply argue that you are a total public servant; you make no distinction between your political and personal life; your life is 'seamless'.

Should it be discovered that you keep your 'donations' in an offshore account and the leftwing pinkoes get upset, don't dignify their howls with an explanation beyond, 'That's the way I chose to do it.'

Let's be frank, here. You should understand why hard-nosed business people hand over chunks of money. They know how the world works. Up and coming entrepreneurs are advised to make a 'contribution' and establish themselves as players. Some prefer to make their 'legitimate political contributions' during an election year. It looks better that way. Some prefer to spread them out over a number of years. Some limit their 'contributions' to a single party; others spread them out over all parties likely to take part in government, covering all the angles.

What matters is that they are seen to be on board, part of the establishment. They can be relied on. Here's the logic politicians traditionally use to justify this kind of thing:

Politicians who have committed themselves to public service, forsaking a life in business – where they could have made fortunes of their own – make it possible for the entrepreneurs to thrive in a stable society. Therefore, the least the entrepreneurs can do is fund those politicians' campaigns.

Entrepreneurs seek no direct return for this. It is, in effect, the price of admission. They are now equals among the lads. They will be expected to cough up on a fairly regular basis. They may or may not get a return on this investment; but they have cast their bread upon the waters.

Mind you, it is slightly more complicated these days, as various scandals forced the political establishment to bring in rules and laws limiting the size and secrecy of donations. If necessary, larger contributions can be broken up so they appear to be made by a variety of individuals. Even when the generosity of wealthy donors is publicised, there is nothing connecting the donation to any purported favour. Wealthy people have a constitutional right to support their chosen party or politician.

Remember: it's one thing for the begrudgers to know what's going on. It's something else for them to prove it.

Politicians with clout will fairly regularly have to make decisions that determine who gets contracts, what gets built, where it gets built and – perhaps – who gets to build it, who gets to fit it out, who gets to provide it with services. People in certain areas of business will probably at some stage be involved in a project that needs a political blessing. An opportunity may arise, or a problem. If they have already established themselves as people who matter, nothing need be said. Perhaps something can be done, perhaps not. Lucky breaks happen to lucky people.

In similar circumstances, should individuals decline a request for a 'legitimate political contribution', and therefore fail to establish themselves as reliable players of the great game, nothing will be said. Unexpected obstacles will appear, contracts won't come through. Unlucky breaks just plain happen.

Perhaps most important of all: donations ensure that certain people have access to politicians. These people give their views on impending legislation. Many of them will never require you to do anything for them. They are happy, and will continue to donate as long as you understand that there are laws and measures that should not be passed. What is *not* done matters as much as what is done.

If leftwing pinkoes want to describe this as corrupt, that is their democratic right. Of course, as your professional cute hoors will point out, if it wasn't for the sacrifices made by people such as yourself, and all the other tribunes of democracy, the leftwing pinkoes wouldn't have the freedom of speech to demonise hardworking democrats.

How to Stop Worrying and Embrace That Tribunal

If you become caught up in a public scandal, don't panic; chances are you can get out of it without too much damage. In some circumstances, the Ben Dunne Strategy – invented when the Big Fella was caught powdering his nose with an illegal substance – might work. You admit everything, without revealing a single fact beyond that which you know they can already prove. You do so wryly, say you feel a fool, express regret for the pain it has caused your family and friends, own up to being a sinner and promise you will seek help. This works only with moral scandals and is damn all use if you've been caught on the wrong side of a brown envelope.

In such a case, the Oireachtas may – with great reluctance – end up having to mount an inquiry of some kind, even a tribunal. Don't feel that your colleagues are having a go at you. A tribunal is the soft option. It allows the politicians put the matter at arms length; it allows the state authorities – the police, the Revenue and so on – continue their respectful attitude towards people with connections. Tribunals may be embarrassing, but they have no power. They can't arrest you or charge you or fine you or ban you or put you in jail for anything they uncover. They are an admission that there are classes of people not amenable to the criminal, disciplinary and regulatory laws, rules and institutions that apply to the rest of us. So, put up with the nosy bastards and be thankful that no matter how blatant your behaviour, criminally inclined people who matter are more likely to ride their camels through the eye of a needle than to end up in the slammer.

In short, stop worrying about the tribunal; embrace it. If the alternative is a criminal investigation, a tribunal is the best thing that can happen to you.

The downside is that you may be called to explain publicly how come you were on the receiving end of several chunky wads of cash. You therefore need to know how to respond should that long thin envelope arrive, with a requirement that you take yourself off to Dublin Castle and explain why you have 116 bank accounts, some of them in your own name.

Being hauled before a tribunal is no fun. You are grilled by very experienced lawyers. Ask around: you will find that the best barrister in town is wholly ruthless, deceitful, greedy and unprincipled. So, hire the shyster before someone else does.

How to Give Evidence at a Tribunal

First, get your barrister on the tribunal. Get him to take the bastards to court and quote reams of obscure case law about this or that, proving to your satisfaction – if not the court's – that the tribunal is exceeding its powers and stomping all over your constitutional rights, not to mention your right to natural justice. This can continue for weeks. With various postponements and appeals, you can drag it out for months, if not years. At dinner parties you can explain with great solemnity how you'd much rather answer the questions; it would be *so* easy to clear your name of the dastardly aspersions being cast upon it, but you have a citizen's duty to defend the constitutional rights of the individual from the intrusiveness of the 'nanny state'. Call the tribunal a 'blunt instrument'. Your peers will shake their heads in sympathy. Some of them – being equally committed to the importance of civil liberties – will ask for the name of your solicitor and hire a fat barrister of their own, with instructions to protect their own constitutional rights.

(The use of the term 'fat barrister' is not derogatory but descriptive. It is an observable fact that the bellies, backsides, chests, necks, chins and jowls of barristers – with few exceptions – expand in direct ratio to the size of their fees. It is truly remarkable to see a barrister emerging from a major case or a tribunal laden down with riches and then to see him grow exponentially in the following months, as though mutating into a different form of life. Only rarely can this phenomenon be ascribed to a glandular complaint. Overpaid and underworked, these people spend far too long at the dinner table, becoming over-acquainted with more fine wines than is good for them.)

One of the curious features of recent years is the appearance on the bench of a small number of judges who give an impression of having a genuine commitment to public service. Such people, perhaps, spent too much time listening to hippy songs in the 1960s and 1970s. Fortunately, however, they are very much a minority. Judges, as a class, come from the ranks of the people who matter and most are very aware of that. They were all appointed by politicians and are aware of the realities of what we like to call 'the real world'. Many of them will have spent some time, as barristers, campaigning for one party or another. Some may have written speeches for young, ambitious politicians who later went on to accept thick wads of cash from bulky men in expensive but ill-fitting suits.

Some have unfulfilled ambitions and are aware that vacancies in the higher courts are also in the gift of politicians, who will always bear in mind that such vacancies must be filled with people who are aware of what is expected of them in 'the real world'. So, you just might get a break. Even if your legal case is threadbare and you have to eventually give evidence to the tribunal, a sympathetic judge may be able to allow you win on one or two points, and that can be helpful, if only in slowing things down.

There are two reasons for slowing things down: the first is that it puts off the evil day when you have to sit up there on the witness stand, with fat barristers employed by the tribunal pushing and prodding at your story, in search of weak points while the gobshites from the media take down your every word.

The second is that if you can drag things out for long enough it is always possible that a crucial witness will die of natural causes.

If you're lucky, the tribunal judge himself may pop his clogs and the whole process will be halted in its tracks, to the relief of freedom-loving individuals everywhere, and their stockbrokers.

However, since you cannot depend on God striking dead an irreplaceable witness, it is as well to be prepared for the dreaded day. Here are some guidelines to help you survive the ordeal.

Smile:

As you walk across the yard at Dublin Castle, let your face light up like you've just heard Ronan Collins call out your sixth number in the Lotto. It is a tradition that witnesses going into and coming out of tribunals behave as though they are being tickled by invisible jesters. Their image consultants have advised them that, however compromising the evidence, they must smile cheerfully and confidently for the cameras.

Whatever you do, don't try to hide from the cameras; don't snarl, don't make obscene gestures or threaten to break anyone's legs. And there is nothing newspapers like better than someone using a newspaper, a jacket or briefcase to hide their face. This makes a great picture and whenever your name comes up in public, even ten or twenty years later, this is the one they will use. Instead, smile. Nod a cheerful hello to the media. Be nice.

The theory is that the detail of your behaviour will quickly be buried in the complications of the next scandal to come along, and what people remember will be the image of you smiling as though you haven't a thing to hide. For this reason, the last twenty yards leading to the door of a tribunal is known as Giggle Alley. It has been scientifically calculated that the gravity of the scandal afflicting the pillars of our society, multiplied by the number of media cameras waiting to photograph them, equals the width of their smiles as they stroll nonchalantly down Giggle Alley.

Volunteer what you cannot conceal:

If you know that the tribunal has information on you, don't wait to be asked about it. Voluntarily turn over your records on this matter. They will get the stuff anyway, so it's best to appear to be cooperating. Never destroy material that you know is duplicated elsewhere – as sure as you do, they'll catch you at it. It is a crime to destroy material that a court or tribunal has ordered you to produce. However, bear in mind that if you have not yet received a court order there is no law to prevent you tidying up your records and disposing of files that unnecessarily take up space. (In fact, we won't take offence if you want to take a break and do a bit of tidying up right now.)

Too much is better than too little:

If you give them the bare minimum from your records they will keep coming after you. Lean the other way. Wheel out every file, the thicker the better, in any way related to anything that might have even a passing connection with the matter under inquiry. If you have hopes that the tribunal might overlook a needle, give them a haystack. Do not hesitate to present the tribunal with huge files of ESB bills from 1982 to 1997; throw in all your office furniture receipts from 1988 onwards, your stationery invoices and hire car bills, your bank statements and credit union dockets, used betting slips and takeaway pizza receipts. Somewhere in there, tuck the stuff you hope they won't notice. It is advisable to go out of your way to collect such trivia, for future use. Deliver all this crap at the same time, as late as possible.

Carefully consider every word you speak:

While the tribunal can't jail you for giving or taking bribes, there is a slight chance you could end up in the Joy for contempt, or for perjury. So, speak very carefully, with great deliberation and with relative honesty – though there's no need to get obsessional about that last bit.

Practise your wiggle-words:

Never give an unqualified answer, particularly when denying something. The bastards may have dug up evidence you thought was shredded. Always throw in 'to the best of my knowledge'. A useful variation is: 'not to my certain knowledge'. And don't forget 'to the best of my recollection'.

If you deny knowing about something and the tribunal produces evidence that you did know, or should have known, you can claim that the matter was 'not fully' within your knowledge, or not to your 'certain' knowledge, and you didn't want to give incomplete or misleading answers to the tribunal – for which, of course, you have the greatest respect. You can, if necessary, point out that you *did* say that you were giving evidence only to the best of your knowledge and recollection. You can't be expected to remember every little detail, particularly when you are being harassed by a bullying barrister.

The object is to mislead and deceive without technically committing perjury, and that requires precision in the use of words.

There are other useful – indeed one might say essential – wiggle-words. These include 'at this time'; and 'in those circumstances'. You can always claim later that something (a) happened at a time other than that to which you were referring when giving evidence; or, (b) the circumstances in which it happened were significantly different.

It may help to scatter the word 'particular' through your evidence, as in 'at that particular time' and 'in those particular circumstances'. It doesn't mean anything, but it provides slightly more wriggle-room.

Commit the following to memory:

'To the *best of my recollection* I received no *such* payment and, furthermore, an examination of my records *of that particular time* reveals that, to *the best of my knowledge*, I never received any *such* payment in *those particular circumstances*.'

Sit in front of a mirror, repeating that sentence slowly, until you have it word perfect. Each of the italicised words increases your wiggle room, and none should be omitted.

Watch how you sit:

Body language is important, for sincerity purposes. Lean forward to emphasise particular points. When you lean back, tilt your head slightly forward and look up through your upper eyelashes towards the fat barrister. This soulful pose is an immense aid in the creation of an impression of sincerity.

Be careful not to 'steeple' your fingers while waiting for the fat barrister to finish his interminable question: it reveals your sense of superiority. And, while that is no doubt justified, it can diminish the impression of sincerity.

(By the way, we hope you appreciate that you're getting a good deal here. For information of this kind, the Bunny Carr School of Applied Sincerity – wherein all sorts of politicians and bulky men with expensive suits learn how to polish their image – would charge you the kind of money better spent stuffing thick brown envelopes.)

You are not a comedian:

Don't make any quips or smart remarks, unless they are agreed following lengthy discussion and consultation with your legal team. If an off-the-cuff smart remark is required, hire any one of a number of professional cute hoors who rent out their wit to advertising agencies, marketing outfits and image consultants, and they will supply you with a selection.

Remember our departed brethren:

You may, in the period since the alleged scandal occurred, have had the good luck to see a dear, close friend shuffle off to his reward. Congratulations. Friends are dear to us; dead friends are priceless. They can, to coin a phrase, come in dead handy. Dead friends can be blamed for just about anything. If the deceased was even marginally connected to the matter being investigated, you can simply claim to have long ago assigned your financial affairs to be dealt with solely by your trusted friend. You are shocked to discover that questions have been raised about the matter at hand. If there is anything you can do to clarify matters, you are very anxious to do so. Unfortunately, your late friend was totally responsible for these affairs and – given his unfortunate passing – you are not in a position to give a definitive answer. While you retain great love and respect for your late friend, and are anxious to see that his good name is not lightly taken, you realise that you have a duty to help the tribunal reach the truth. Then, attach as much of the crap as possible to your late friend.

You'll find that some people are squeamish about the ethics of blaming the dear departed. However, your dead friend would no doubt be happy to take the rap – if he was a true friend at all.

Be precise:

If you are hemmed in, answer only the precise question you have been asked.

For example: if you are ever questioned about allegations that you've been having carnal relations with a sheep named Constance, and you have in fact been on intimate terms with a pig named Garrett, you must bristle with indignation and state simply and firmly that the allegation is a total invention.

If pressed:

Many fat barristers are cowards. They have to put the hard questions, but they back off if you give them an excuse. If, for example, you are pressed on your relationship with animals, look the fat barrister straight in the eye and state firmly and clearly that you never met a sheep named Constance, that you never had a relationship with a sheep called Constance, nor with any other sheep, nor with any sheep-like creature. State this on your word of honour, on your child's life, on the memory of your dead father. Here you may clear your throat and pause a few seconds. Your own fat barrister will be primed to leap to his feet and ask for an adjournment while you recover your emotional balance, but you should wave him away and insist on continuing. That always looks good. If asked about Garrett the pig, merely refer to your previous answer and, if pressed, shake your head slowly, sigh deeply, as though saddened by the opposing fat barrister's hard neck, and say you intend to treat that question with the contempt it deserves.

Make them work for it:

Fat barristers will ask simple questions, then pause expectantly – inviting you to expand. Unless you know that they already have evidence, volunteer nothing. If they ask if it's true that you received a thick brown envelope from Larry on Wednesday 12 April, and you know they have evidence that you did, it's best to say 'Yes'. There's no law that says you have to tell them that you got brown envelopes from Larry on Tuesday 11 and Thursday 13, as well. And don't volunteer the information that at around the same time you also received brown envelopes from Curly and Moe. Admit only what they can prove.

Be indignant:

If they know about the envelope the chances are they

know it was full of money, so if they ask what was in the envelope you're going to have to own up. Put your indignation on the record. It won't get you very far but it goes down well at the golf club. The recommended maximum for speaking in your sincerest tones about privacy and the rights of the individual is two minutes; if you continue for much longer it will look like you're trying to avoid the issue. Do your indignant bit, then say there was money in the envelope. *State* this firmly, proudly, to avoid any impression that you're *admitting* it. When they ask why you accepted money from a person whose business interests could be affected by your decisions, say that since the very notion that you would do anything wrong is so absurd, it never crossed your mind that there might be cynical people out there who would draw outrageous conclusions from such an innocent transaction.

When they ask why you thought Larry the businessman would want to thrust money in the direction of a politician whose decisions could affect his business, state calmly that it was obvious to you that Larry saw it as his duty to support the democratic process. Say that you assumed that since Ireland had been good to Larry, he felt the need to 'give something back'.

Disregard any giggles from the back of the room. There are always a few leftwing pinkoes mocking and sneering. Don't let them put you off your stride.

You may even – if you feel up to it – make a little speech about how fine men (and women) died to ensure our right to be governed democratically, and you always believed it to be an essential part of democracy that we – and this applies, by God, to each and every one of us – have the right to support in whatever way we can those we believe to be best qualified to govern this great little nation. Feel free to denounce the 'cynics who always knock down, who never build up'. Here's a good line: 'I don't apologise for my patriotism.'

Watch out:

Larry may well have turned over, or 'Dunlopped'. He may be cooperating with the bastards. They may have traced the money, they may have found hidden bank accounts, they might have something else on him, and he might be doing a deal with the Criminal Assets Bureau or the Revenue. You should try to clarify this before you give evidence. Of course, the tribunal may issue an instruction that you do not contact other witnesses, in which case you must not phone Larry. Get your wife to make the call. If necessary, meet in some private place, maybe a flat borrowed from your girlfriend's neighbour. Right away, make light of it all, crack a joke about how you bet these tribunal clowns don't know the half of it, and try to get Larry to say something incriminating about himself. If he speaks freely, you can be pretty sure he's not wired for sound. If both of you can pull together the bones of a credible story, well and good. If Larry is at all reticent or hesitant, you may have to conclude that he's been got at and he's wearing a wire. There's no point being a stand-up guy if it looks like the little shit has already sold you down the river, so feel free to rat him out, as long as you get a trade-off from the CAB, the Revenue, or the tribunal's fat barrister.

Honesty is the best policy:

Assuming that Larry doesn't fall apart like a wet tissue – in which case it's every man for himself and the first one to make a deal is the winner – you have two objectives:

1. To get off the stand without admitting anything
2. To avoid falling into the trap of committing a subsidiary offence, such as perjury or contempt.

Even if you have something major to hide – tax dodging, bribe-taking, whatever – it is extremely dangerous to lie: you must never, ever, ever, *ever* take that option. Ireland has weak laws against brown envelope culture; the tax authorities are usually open to a deal whereby you pay a financial penalty and walk away; many judges are tolerant of certain offences they might well have committed themselves, so they'll give you a break if they can; your fat barrister can quite often be accommodated in finding a loophole.

In short, you'll get away easily with tax evasion and bribery, but judges are stuffy, self-important people who get upset if you make your contempt too obvious. They have hang-ups about perjury, unless you are a fellow member of the Bar, in which case they will extend you the usual professional courtesy. So, unless you are a fat barrister, perjury is a somewhat dangerous tactic. The record shows that the state is extremely unlikely to prosecute someone of your status for perjury; however, there's been so much of it that the public is quite bitter about it and a token bad guy might at any time be nominated to take the heat. A jail sentence is not out of the question. Even worse, if you are caught perjuring yourself, there is a possibility that the tribunal will make you pay your own legal costs, which is a bummer, given the price of fat barristers. There is, if you think long and hard enough, some deceitful form of words that will allow you to squirm out of any corner, no matter how tight, without committing perjury.

Remember (or, rather, don't):

The most important words in your defence armoury are these: 'I don't recall.' There may be a time when your back is to the wall and the other side's fat barrister is relentless. You have to answer but you dare not tell the truth. At that stage say, 'I don't recall', and say it as often as necessary. It may, in the circumstances, be self-evidently absurd to claim you don't remember something. People may laugh openly, the fat barrister may sneer and the judge may frown, but they can't look inside your head. They cannot *prove* that you remember something.

Fallback:

Your ultimate fallback position, should they make a connection between you and a dodgy donation, is that no favours were sought or given. It is virtually impossible for the snoopers to connect a financial donation and a favour.

As long as you haven't left a piece of paper lying around with the inscription: 'Thanks for the financial donation, I'll arrange the favour immediately', you can fervently claim that the donation was unconnected with the favourable decision. On the one hand, a genuine political donation; on the other, a decision made for worthy reasons wholly unconnected with the donation. There's no connection between them.

No one will believe you, but without unassailable evidence of a connection, you will not be prosecuted.

To sum up:

Stay cool, hang loose, admit nothing. Speak with precision; practise your wiggle-words; do not volunteer any information; if necessary, sell out your accomplices before they sell you out; don't forget that you can deceive without committing perjury; you must never, *ever* lie on oath. And remember not to remember.

If all this fails: take a deep breath, look the fat barrister straight in the eye – and lie.

Life After Politics

How will you measure your success in Irish politics? Some measure it by the number and the seniority of the positions they reached in the course of a career. Some by the number of first preference votes they stroked.

Some quietly tot up the useful measures they helped to get onto the statute books, even if only by suggesting them to a minister over a pint in the Members' Bar. Some genuinely believe that perpetually hogging information and using it to put their constituents under a compliment – that may be repaid at the ballot box – is political success.

Some look at the dimensions of their bank balance, and reflect that in no other business could they have been as financially successful.

Some don't count their career a success unless they manage to pass the seat on to a son or daughter.

Some count their offshore accounts, their second and third homes, the favours they have done and the favours done in return. They measure the size of the financial legacy they will pass on to their kids. They may live in dread of certain information coming to light, but they have scant fear that they will ever face the laws they helped – as legislators – to bring in.

There is another measure of political success, one that we must mention only for the sake of comprehensiveness. It assumes that politics, rather than being a business, is about developing a society's resources and distributing them fairly, while protecting the rights of the individual. It assumes that those active in politics will offer an analysis of how society works and seek to win democratic support for the conclusions they draw from that analysis.

It assumes that holders of political jobs, rather than being careerists, should be genuinely representative and accountable. It assumes that political success is not measured in the advantages accumulated by an individual but in the collective progress of the community the individual represents.

It assumes that a democracy involves people in the continuing management of their community: they are citizens, rather than 'voters' who get to mark a piece of paper every few years.

This way of thinking is strictly for leftwing pinko losers and is not recommended for serious politicians who live in 'the real world'.

However you measure success – whether you aim no higher than the backbenches or you hope to be graced with a Mercedes under your backside – some day it will all be over. You will lose your seat or you will retire on your generous pension. You must remember that there is life after politics. It is called: appointment to the boards of private sector companies.

There are companies that like to rent a degree of status by paying former politicians to sit at the high table during AGMs, nodding solemnly, chuckling at the CEO's quips and applauding when the boss finishes a speech. It stands to reasons that politicians who have been particularly understanding of the needs of such companies are more likely to be invited onto the board. Keep that in mind from the outset of your career.

Only a small percentage of former politicians bother to take advantage of a political afterlife. For most, the career is lucrative, the pension is generous, and if they have built up a little offshore pot of money, or a rewarding sideline, so much the better. Some, however, can't bear leaving the limelight.

There was a time when political retirement opened up the possibility of running for the Presidency, a position that is 'above politics', but that's almost certainly out of your reach. The position is now reserved for younger, earnest, high-profile females in search of a career stepping-stone. You'll need to try elsewhere.

If you remain a backbencher for your entire career, the options are limited. If you attain higher office, there are various post-retirement possibilities. An MEP might drop dead from eating too many rich sauces at EU free lunches, freeing up a position that requires a clapped-out but recognisable candidate. Your media contacts might wangle you a newspaper column, from which you can advise the nation. Nobody reads columns written by ex-politicians. Such columns are always terminally boring, without exception; there are dictionaries where 'newspaper column by former politician' is given as the primary definition of the word boring. However, newspapers like to have them; they add solemnity to a page.

You could find post-politics work as a consultant, becoming a part-time professional cute hoor, working the interface between politics and business. You know where the bodies are buried; you know the government departments, the ministerial advisers and the civil servants. You know who is effective and who is a time-server; you know which adviser has the minister's ear and which is the office joke. You know who to phone, who to take to lunch, who is open to influence and who is a stick-in-the-mud.

If that sounds too much like work, settle for a directorship or two. As a director, your duties are even lighter than those of a TD, and the constituency you have to suck up to is much smaller, which leaves oodles of time for golf. Remember, during your political career, to take the trouble to impress the right people and when the time comes you may be offered a place as an ornament on one or more boards.

The significant 'emoluments' that help fatten your income are not to be sneezed at, but it's the prestige that counts. You are still needed; your worth is recognised. After a career of selfless public service, you are demonstrating that – had you felt like it – you could have had a glittering career at the front line of business and commerce. After all, it's not everyone has the *gravitas* it takes to sit at the high table, nodding solemnly and laughing in just the right places.

Onward and Upward

Off you go, then. You're as ready as we can make you. From nomination to election, to high office, and retirement, and – if you're lucky – a seat on the board. Along the way, should you choose, you may take the occasional walk on the wild side. Very few of those who do so have been caught, very few have had to stroll down Giggle Alley for a date with a tribunal.

It's a rewarding career, the politics business. Power is limited, but real enough. There is some fame: numbers of people will fawn over you, but not anyone you'd want to be seen with in public. The money is good. The perks are limitless. There's lots of time off. But you will be unable to resist holding one more clinic, canvassing one more shopping centre or attending one more funeral, for fear that some ambitious bastard is quietly undermining your power base. In short, politics has its pros and its cons, like any other business, but it offers certain opportunities to those who are less inhibited than they need be by scruple, qualm and doubt.

The naïve may chatter about idealism. We who live in the real world know that you must not ask what you can do for your country; that your country is more than capable of coming up with lists of things it expects you to do for it.

The romantic may prattle about cynicism. We who live in the real world know that Romantic Ireland is dead and gone; its resting place has been bought on the cheap by a consortium that includes two tax exiles, a bent solicitor and a former TD with extensive business interests in Eastern Europe. Planning permission having been obtained by bribery, the cemetery is to be 'developed' as a theme park named Celtic Delight. A file was sent to the DPP, who decided not to press charges.

Perhaps, after all, you will have second thoughts. Politics feeds the ego and the bank account but it's not an easy life. You may not have the necessary mindless ambition. You may have an excess of scruple.

Walk away, if you must. But, remember, with Pericles: 'Just because you are not interested in politics doesn't mean that politics is not interested in you.'